MAKE

C000109463

Dear Cameron,

Keep fit &
be more purple!

Marit X

MAKE THEIR DAY

Make Their Day

Awesome Ways To WOW
Your Customers Every Time

Marie Cross

MAKE THEIR DAY

Text Copyright © Marie Cross 2019

Marie Cross has asserted her right in accordance with the Copyright Designs and Patents Act 1988 to be identified as the author of this work.

All rights reserved

No part of this publication may be lent, resold, hired out or reproduced in any form or by any means without prior written permission from the author and publisher. All rights reserved.
Copyright © 3P Publishing

First published in 2019 in the UK

3P Publishing
C E C, London Road
Corby
NN17 5EU

A catalogue number for this book is available from the British Library

ISBN 978-1-911559-69-6

Cover design: Marie-Louise O'Neill

To my parents – Mary & Roy

Who I inherited my incredible work ethic from and who taught me the value of serving others, having good manners and being a GEM (Going the Extra Mile),

To my boys - Tom, Dan & Joe

You're all MAD - you Make A Difference in your own unique way every day. I couldn't be prouder of the 3 of you if my whole life depended on it.

To my husband, David

Who is my EVERYTHING…

My rock, my confidante, my best friend, my soul mate, my trusted advisor, my teacher, my therapist AND my kick-ass boss!

MAKE THEIR DAY

Contents:

MAKE THEIR DAY

Foreword – by Nigel Botterill

In the movie *Any Given Sunday*, Al Pacino plays American football coach Tony D'Amato. Up against it and trailing at half time in a critical game, Pacino gives one of the best speeches in Hollywood history.

"The inches we need are all around us," he explains. "It's the little things that make the difference."

What Marie Cross has done with this book is compress 100 yards of inches into a single digestible volume.

And these are inches that individually and collectively can and will help you and your team to win at business. More specifically, to win at serving your customers.

"Life's a game of inches..." Pacino tells his team. "…the margins are so small, but the inches we need are everywhere around us".

For business owners, he could have been talking about this book.

"And when we add up all those inches, that's what makes the difference between winning and losing ..." Pacino ends passionately, as the hearts of his team beat faster and they roar out onto the pitch.

There may not be quite as much testosterone in your office as you work through this incredibly useful book, but the impact will be no less great.

MAKE THEIR DAY

What you hold in your hand really can make the difference between winning and losing.

Between living and dying.

Because that's what customer service does for a business.

It's all a game of inches...and this book is full of 'em.

Nigel Botterill

Founder, Entrepreneurs Circle

April 2019

Introduction

I've always been passionate (some say obsessed) about customer service – since I was 12 years of age, in fact. I started my career in helping and serving others in 1974, when I took on a Saturday job at my local hairdressers in South London. Slave labour was commonplace back then, yet I was more than pleased to be working at Babette's with a wage of £3.75 for a full day on my feet with very little down-time, because my take-home pay was always at least double, if not triple that amount each week, due to the fabulous tips I used to get – presumably, for looking after customers so well!

I developed OCD during the early days of working as a Saturday girl and it was a condition I was extremely proud and grateful for, because it served me extremely well – and continues to do so all these years on! OCD is in my blood and runs through my DNA, which I now know I inherited from both my parents – and I'll remain eternally thankful to them both.

Having OCD from such a young age taught me so many positive and powerful lessons about the human race – how being polite and welcoming upon meeting someone for the first time was such an important thing to be, and why appearing genuinely interested in what people had to say and really listening to them was a really smart thing to do. OCD also taught me to empathise and respect others and stand tall and proud in my position as a Brand Ambassador (although I had no idea in 1974 that's what I was), except I knew it was important to represent my boss's salon in a professional and friendly way, especially when anyone walked into the reception area or approached the front desk.

I also recognised from those early days of living with OCD, that people will forget what you say to them and even what you do for them (even if you are a real GEM and Go the Extra Mile) but they'll never, ever forget how you make them *feel.* I kinda guessed it was a good thing to make other people **feel** special and important and cared for, even if I was feeling a little insignificant in the grand scheme of things! I understood, even at that tender age of 12, that working within a service environment meant my entire focus and energy and attention would always need to be on the person I was serving – and I needed to do everything in my power to ensure a PME for them on each and every occasion they interacted with me.

It took me another 10 years to realise that PME stood for a **P**ositive **M**emorable **E**xperience

Living very positively and happily with OCD isn't for everyone – I get that.

Some people don't want to be MAD (Make A Difference) or live on GAS (Give A Sh*t) and I get that too. Some people just want to do a job, get paid and/or rewarded appropriately, go home and live their life… and that's cool, although it's not the way I ever lived or plan to live my life. Still, as they say in Yorkshire *"there's nowt so queer as folk"* and as we all know, we only have one thing in common, which is we're all different! "Each to their own" as they say!

Just doing a job and getting paid commensurate with the effort of doing it would never have been enough for me. Indeed, it actually wasn't enough for me back in 2011 when my business was on the verge of collapsing. I took on several freelance projects *and* some voluntary work with my local senior school (more to maintain my sanity than anything else) where my financial reward was pitiful. Ordinarily, I wouldn't have put my coat on for the daily fee I got freelancing, but desperate times called for desperate measures. And yet… I can honestly say that those dark days of having to do whatever it took to get back on my feet and rebuild my business were some of the brightest, most positive, most rewarding days of my entire career – of my life even! My OCD was almost out of control during this time and I couldn't have been happier that was the case.

I was a real GEM and went the extra mile every time. I knew what it took to be MAD and live on GAS as a means of showing up and standing out from the crowd, in order to get back on my feet and get that one step ahead of everyone else in my field. I hadn't even come across *Purple Cow* by Seth Godin back then, although I instinctively knew, having had OCD for so very long, that I was indeed that Purple Cow in *my* particular field. That was the reason I'd achieved the reputation I had, the respect and regard for what I did, and the admiration of many for how I'd continued to get back up if I was ever knocked down, from my slave labour days back in 1974 right up until today, in 2019, when my OCD is probably at its absolute best - and boy, I'm thrilled about that, because it means I'll continue to show up and stand out!

So this book is all about my journey of living with OCD and being a Purple Cow. If you work within a service environment, where you're representing your organisation on the front line as a Brand Ambassador (by phone, face-to-face or even via the electronic word) *and* you relish the idea of being MAD, living on GAS and acting like a Purple Cow, then this book is absolutely for you!

It ain't rocket science you know! Small things can make a *big* difference when it comes to serving others – in both business and life and I for one, at just 5ft tall, am standing proud (*and* tall) to **be** the difference that **makes** the difference when it comes to WOWing customers with that PME, in order to get and stay that vital one step ahead of **my** competition.

Will you join me – and be more OCD?

Whatever you decide – here's to your continued success!

Marie X

PS. You'll have to read the book now to understand what OCD *really* stands for…

> *We cannot reach new horizons until we're prepared to lose sight of the shore!*

Becoming a service legend – It pays to care!

- It costs five times more to attract a new customer than to maintain an existing one.

- If a customer receives good service, he or she will tell five people on average, yet if a customer receives bad service, he or she will tell 11 people on average.

- Until recently, only 1 in 26 people in the UK on average bothered to complain at the point of something going wrong – the rest just churn! But the world of complaining is changing – more than a third (36%) of people are now using social media to escalate a complaint.

- 42% of those complaining via social media expect a response within 60 minutes!

- If a customer has a major problem resolved satisfactorily, 82% will do business with you again and almost half of consumers (48%)

said they would be happy with just an apology!

- If a customer has a major problem but remains silent, 91% will not do business with you again.

- Customers who have a problem, which is effectively resolved are four times more loyal than customers who have never had a problem – and more than half of them (52%) think "more highly" of the company that handles their complaint effectively.

- One loyal customer is worth 12 new customers, because they spend an average 300% more!

- 68% of customers who choose to move their business or loyalty elsewhere do so due to a "lack of care or contact" by their Provider.

- 86% of customers would pay 25% more for a better customer experience.

- 20% of your customer base will spend more money with you if you make the opportunity available e.g. offering add-ons, premium products, upgrades etc.

- 84% of customer perception is emotional. Opinions and views and judgements about the service a customer receives are all based on how customers feel about their experience and emotions are processed 24 times faster than rationale and logic!

- We never get a second chance to create a great first impression – and people form their views and opinions of us within the first 4 to 34 seconds face-to-face (based only on how we "appear" to the person) and the first 4 to 14 seconds over the phone (based on what and how we speak).

- 46% of customer complaints are resolved slower than customers expect or demand

- Email has overtaken the telephone as the most commonly used customer service channel in 2018

- 60% of customers now expect a response within 24 hours of contacting you via email

- Women are 50% more likely than men to seek assistance via social media

- Millennials will wait twice as long as older customers to speak to a customer service advisor by phone

- UK customers rate their top three customer-service irritants as follows:
    - 56% of us are most annoyed by automated telephone systems.
    - 52% of us find annoying "hold" music – well, annoying!
    - 48% of us are irritated by rude staff.

References: Institute of Customer Service (ICS) 'State of Customer Satisfaction in UK' Report 2018/Oracle "Customer Experience Impact" Report 2015 Which? Top 10 Customer Irritations Report 2015/Awards International Report 2017/Gartner's 2017 / Customer Experience Magazine 2018 / Revolution Events Ltd 2018

We can never be more than we believe is possible, so believe in possibilities!

The Success Recipe –
the Difference that makes the Difference!

There have been hundreds of research studies, books, seminars and courses discussing what it takes to achieve excellence and reach the pinnacle of your game. I'd like to introduce you to what is the most important lesson in this book: The Success Recipe.

There are many shining examples of The Success Recipe in both business and life. There are the obvious gurus, like Sir Richard Branson, Lord Sugar and Tony Robbins. Then there's Lord Sugar's trusted aide Karren Brady, Holly Tucker and Sophie Cornish, founders of notonthehighstreet.com and *Dragon's Den* star Deborah Meaden.

There are the not-so-well-known, yet equally successful gurus, like my kick-ass business mentor Nigel Botterill, founder of the *Entrepreneurs Circle*; Lindsey Agness, my NLP teacher, friend and guide, author of several books and the first female master trainer of NLP in the UK; and Justine Roberts, co-founder of the internet giant *Mumsnet*, recently voted the seventh most powerful woman in the UK by BBC viewers alongside her business partner Carrie Longton.

All these people share the three key elements of The Success Recipe – they have the **knowledge, skills** and **attitude** to guarantee they reach the pinnacle of their game.

Let's take a look at these three key elements in more detail:

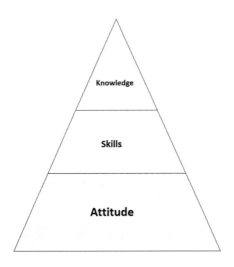

1. Knowledge

The first ingredient that we need in place to ensure our success is **knowledge**. We must know about the job we perform, the work we do and the living we're making.

So what knowledge do you need to have in your toolkit to be successful?

- **Company knowledge**: your position in the marketplace, your products and services, your company's infrastructure etc.

- **Technical knowledge**: your systems and processes, protocols, policies and procedures that need to be followed.

- **Job knowledge**: understanding what your role involves, what's expected of you, your KPIs and targets etc.

- **Customer knowledge**: understanding your customers' likes and dislikes, buying patterns, knowing who your target market is and who your customer avatar is.

- **Self-knowledge**: What are the strengths and attributes that *you* have to offer to your organisation and your colleagues? What do *you* bring to the table that increases the whole team's chances of success?

Knowledge alone is not going to secure our success, since knowledge isn't power unless it's used properly, artfully and skilfully. So our second ingredient we must have in our toolkit is a **skill-set**

2. Skills

So what **skills** would be useful in that kit bag of *yours* that will enable you to impart all this knowledge in a coherent, fluid and skilful way, to increase your chances of success?

- **Communication skills:** verbal and vocal, written, listening and questioning skills.

- **Interpersonal skills:** building rapport, mirroring and matching others, presentation skills.

- **Customer service or sales skills:** negotiating, influencing, decision-making or problem-solving skills.

- **Technical skills:** IT, accountancy, numeracy skills etc.

Skills, like knowledge, are referred to as "enablers" in the Success Recipe. They relate to our ability to do a good job and increase our chances of success, although both ingredients are generally things that are taught to us, unless we have some previous experience to bring with us to the role.

This is a bit of a blow to realise, because that suggests that two-thirds of our success depends on an external source – something, or someone, teaching us in order to be a success. In a worst-case scenario, we may have to teach ourselves when new in a job and starting from square one – which is where vital ingredient number three comes into its own!

In order to be a true success in *anything* we choose to do, we need more than a bag-full of knowledge and skills – we need an **attitude** that's full of all the right qualities to ensure our success and of course, those qualities are all down to you!

3. Attitude

You'll be pleased to know that the most important ingredient in the Success Recipe is you! No one teaches **you** to be **you** except **you**. You make the difference to your success in both business *and* life.

This is the base and foundation upon which the other elements can be built. So the most critical ingredient in this Recipe of Success is our **attitude**. We need the right attitude, behaviours and characteristics in our personality, as well as the right mindset to set our direction on our journey to success.

> *Whether you think you can or whether you think you can't, either way – you're right!*

Attitudes are contagious, so make sure yours is worth catching

Attitude is everything! It's the foundation upon which our success is built, and it is what separates you from your competition.

People buy from or buy into someone who sounds positive and upbeat, interested and interesting, not from somebody who sounds negative, or gives the impression that they don't want to be there.

All those happy-clappy trainers and motivational speakers tell us that to secure our success all we need to do is stay positive, smile, to practise a constant positive mental attitude and all will be well. That's a little easier said than done though, isn't it? They clearly haven't worked on a front line like you or I. Sometimes when we've had just about as much as we can stomach in a day, we don't feel particularly chirpy or positive or customer focused and remaining upbeat can be tough.

Let's take a look at some of the things that can chip away at our positivity...

Mine are being hungry (my mood definitely drops when I'm hungry, that's for sure) and those daily BMWs (blamers, moaners, and whingers). Those are the customers and colleagues who bleed you dry and suck every ounce of energy out of you, blaming everything and everyone rather than accepting any responsibility themselves!

Lazy colleagues or rude, ignorant customers can be another "attitude buster" for some people and sometimes, personal worries or financial issues can cause our moods to wane.

So what can we do about all these things? There will always be events that affect our mood, or people who wind us up the wrong way – isn't this just life? S**t happens as they say!

I love the adage *"accept the things that you cannot change and change the things that you cannot accept"*.

We can't change the event or the person; we can't make a difficult customer change their behaviour towards us, or make the rain suddenly stop because we're fed up of suffering with that SAD syndrome and we can't turn our colleague into a super-supportive, helpful team player.

So let's stop festering on things that are out of our control and start working on doing something about those things that are within our control. It's not **what** happens that matters, it's how we **respond** to what happens and it's important to have a few tips, techniques and strategies for responding in a way that will get you back on track with your PMA, so that you can make the most of that vital ingredient, which is **you**!

Accept that attitude is a choice – and it's **your** choice! You cannot be knocked off kilter unless **you** give up on your personal power and control – so let's take a look at some hints and tips for getting our attitude in order and staying on track, in order to succeed as Brand Ambassadors on our front line.

Here are our top 10 tips for maintaining a positive mental attitude (PMA).

1. **Have anchors**. They can be visual, auditory, kinaesthetic or sensory; photos, stress balls, your favourite song, or a visual image in your mind of your favourite holiday spot, or your best night out ever that you can recreate in your mind's eye in a flash.

2. **Smile**. It is an outward sign of inner enthusiasm and if you're feeling good inside you ought to be letting your face know it!

Dopamine is released when we smile and that causes all sorts of positive vibes and feelings, so feel free to get hooked on the happiness drug.

3. **Check out your body position and posture**. Sitting straight and forward, or even standing up if you're dealing with one of those difficult customers on the 'phone, is a great way to create a positive internal state and it helps us to feel taller, more confident, more assertive and generally more positive.

4. **Roosevelt's Rule**. Eleanor Roosevelt, wife of American President Theodore Roosevelt, implied that no one has the right, the power, or the control to affect your attitude without your permission. Remember that attitude is **your** choice. This rule should be on the wall board or notice board of every front-line operation on the planet, in my opinion.

5. **Mix in Success**. Do what does not come naturally. Go find someone who appears to be having a great day, is looking and feeling in a good mood, is smiley and happy and upbeat and snatch some of their good vibes. We're all energy and energy transfers and attitudes are contagious, so make sure that yours is one

worth catching. If it isn't, then go find somebody whose attitude *is* worth catching!

6. **Keep it in Perspective**. We're serving a customer, not a life sentence! No one died (hopefully) and we're always going to have to deal with the odd person who we'd rather not – it's the nature of the beast and it comes with the territory, so let's keep things in perspective. We should never ever become so busy making a living that we forget to make a life. That is not to say that we shouldn't give the job our 100% attention and focus during our working day, but it also doesn't mean that we should devote our entire life to it either. Work-life balance is still not very well understood or executed sadly – and it needs to be.

7. **The Fake-It Technique:** This is one of my all-time favourite tips for maintaining a PMA. When you learn to **act** as if something quite remarkable can happen, you move closer to it becoming your reality. As an example, you may recall the soap drama *EastEnders* and the character Arthur Fowler, who suffered with acute depression. The actor, Bill Treacher, played the part so brilliantly that in real life he started to actually suffer from depression and asked to

be written out of the soap for fear of his health. When you practise the Fake-It Technique, when you act as if you are having a good day, the customer is going to accept your suggestions, or you are going to meet target this month, the closer you'll get to this becoming your reality!

8. **Reframe Negative Self-Talk.** Psychological research tells us that we talk to ourselves at a rate of around 600 words per minute. Professor Winston, the great expert paediatrician, proved that 78% of what we communicate to our children up to adulthood is negative. Is it any wonder, therefore, that as adults 75% of our self-talk is negative? Just stop and listen to yourself. Are you being supportive and helpful to your thoughts and feelings about your worth and your ability to do a good job? We rarely rise above our own opinion of ourselves, and generally speaking, that opinion tends to be very low. So build a bridge and get over it – move out of your own way and start talking more positively to yourself about yourself!

9. **The Screen Idea.** Complete this exercise in a quiet place, away from noise. Close your eyes and think about a situation that has upset you and experience it fully – see what you saw,

hear what you heard and really feel what you felt as you re-live that experience. Now imagine projecting that image up onto a cinema screen in your mind and start to change the qualities of the image... tone down the colours to black and white. Stop any movement and make it into a still. Then turn the sounds down. Imagine the screen is moving further and further away and notice how the feelings start to reduce their intensity. When the screen has moved further away and is the size of an A4 sheet of paper, imagine taking it in your hands, crumpling it up tightly into a ball and then hold out your hand and imagine an elastic band between your thumb and forefinger. Hold the ball against the band and then pull it back and ping it off into the distance. Out of sight, out of mind.

10. **The Mental Enema Technique**. Think of a situation where someone has caused you to feel angry, frustrated, disappointed or upset. Take an A4 sheet of paper and a very large crayon, or a flipchart pen and write down all the negative feelings and thoughts about that person or that situation. Don't hold back. Now, tear the piece of paper into as many pieces as you can, toss the bits into a wastepaper bin and wipe your hands clean to

rid yourself of those awful feelings once and for all.

To conclude this section on attitude busters and builders, I'd like to share with you the most valuable little tip of all. A 1% idea that can have a 100% impact on your attitude.

It's *the* formula for success when it comes to staying positive and on track!

$$E + R = O$$

Here's how it works. The E stands for the **Event** (a rude customer, aggressive prospect, whiny colleague and so on). The **Event** is simply life – it's all that "stuff" that happens day in day out, that you and I have no control over. The R of the formula has two parts – we can either choose to do what is perfectly normal and natural and we can **React** to this event, or we can find a way to press the pause button, think things through for a moment and **Respond** to this event. Whichever R we choose, we will have an **Outcome** – this is the O part of the formula. Dependent on which R we've chosen, that outcome is likely to be either a negative or a positive one.

However, here's what most of us have missed when it comes to applying this little formula – we don't have any control over the event and we also don't have any control over the outcome, because that's wholly determined by which R we choose! The only part of the formula that you and I have total control over is the R, because we can **choose** how we'll deal with what happens to us – do we give a knee-jerk **Reaction** or do we give a considered **Response**?

Choose your R wisely. Find a way to press that pause button so that you take a moment to think through in a more considered way what might be the best way to deal with a problem.

My advice to you here is to start with the end in mind, as Stephen Covey taught us, in his best-selling book *'The 7 Habits of Highly Effective People.'* Ask yourself, *"What's the best outcome I can have here? What would make me feel good about this experience that I'm having?"* You'll find it much easier to press that pause button to then access all those little in-the-moment hints and tips that we've looked at for getting your attitude back in check.

> *Chains of habit are too light to be felt until they are too heavy to be broken!*

Developing the RA-O Factor!

Being a Brand Ambassador means you must take full **Responsibility**, **Accountability** and **Ownership** for everything that you say and do on behalf of the company you represent. This may mean having to take the rap for someone else's error or having to accept blame for another department's mistake from time to time.

Even when the situation has had absolutely nothing to do with you, it's a responsibility that we must face up to if we are to represent our brand in the most positive and appropriate way.

Does a customer care whether it was your fault that something went wrong? Of course not, they only want one thing: **action**. They want to know that someone within the company is going to take the **responsibility**, the **accountability** and the **ownership** for sorting things out and reaching a resolution.

It's vital that you live and breathe the RA-O Factor every day in every way with everyone you engage with, whether you're on the phone, face-to-face or communicating through the written word. This means being 100% responsible for everything that happens (or doesn't happen) in order to ensure a positive and memorable experience for your customers and prospects.

How do you live and breathe the RA-O Factor? How does a true Brand Ambassador behave at those times when "poop hits fan" and there is a disgruntled customer to deal with? One simple way is to apologise *on behalf of* the person or department or your company, to prove to the other person that *you* are prepared to live and breathe that RA-O Factor. So be sure to take full Responsibility, Accountability and Ownership for everything that you say and do in the name of your company, because it's proof that you're a true Brand Ambassador.

> *The secret of success –*
> *do what's right, do it right, do it now!*

Study of Communication
(Mehrabian's Model)

Now we're going to look at how we can improve, develop and enhance the key elements of our communication.

In the early 1970s, Dr Albert Mehrabian, an Iranian psychologist, produced some fascinating research documented in his book, *Silent Messages*, proving that we human beings communicate in three fundamental ways:

1. **Visually** – through our dress and appearance; through body language – eye contact, facial expressions, hand movements, gestures etc. and through our posture and physical positioning.

2. **Verbally** – through the actual words we speak, the content of the actual conversation that we're having.

3. **Vocally** – through the way in which we communicate – how we sound in our vocal tone and pitch, inflection, the rise and fall of

the voice, volume, pace and pausing rate and the overall clarity of our sound.

Mehrabian's original study proved that when human beings are communicating for the **first time** in a face-to-face setting, those three key elements of our communication have a varying impact on the person's experience of us and the judgements and decisions they then form in the first three minutes of interaction when **first impressions** are created.

If you think about Mehrabian's Model as a circle of communication representing 100%, if you were meeting someone for the first time, what percentage would you attribute to the person's visual, verbal and vocal communication in terms of the **impact** each of these elements had on you when forming your initial impression of them?

Mehrabian's study shows that the **visual** element represents 55% of the impact. We make a snap judgement within the first 4 to 34 seconds, but we then spend the rest of those three minutes searching for affirmation and confirmation that our instinct in those first 4 to 34 seconds was right! It isn't always right of course, but we never forget that first impression of the other person – and as we know, they don't get a second chance to create one!

The **vocal** element represents 38%, proving the adage, *"It ain't what you say, it's the way that you say it – that's what yields results!"*

This leaves a tiny 7% for the **verbal** element – the actual words that we use, so our actual conversations have very little impact in terms of the other person's impression of us in a first-time meeting.

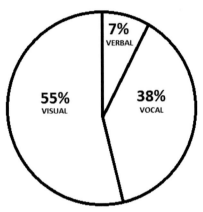

Face to face communication

So how does Mehrabian's Model translate when we're communicating with prospects and customers for the very first time over a *telephone*?

With only two key elements of communication available to impact our customer's experience of us, it's quite a different story.

29

Unlike face-to-face, where people will form those snap judgements in the first 4 to 34 seconds, on the telephone, it'll happen within the first 4 to 14 seconds of us engaging with them. *What* we say and *how* we say it in those critical first few seconds is therefore key! Our verbal element now has to have over four times more impact than if we were communicating the *same* message face-to-face, so we need to start choosing our words much more carefully, remembering that words paint pictures, so we need to ensure that we're using language that is positive, impactful and influences our customer in the right way.

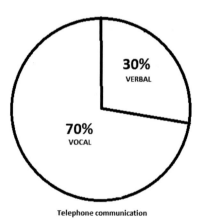

Telephone communication

Our vocal element has to have **almost double** the impact over the phone – and the quality of our sound, our vocal tone and inflection, our volume and pace and overall clarity will have a much bigger effect on our customer's experience.

So let's take a look at the verbal element of our communication and how we can develop a language of influence, avoiding words and phrases that don't have the desired impact on our customers and prospects.

> *An optimist is a person who sees a green light everywhere. The pessimist sees only the red light. But the truly wise person is colour blind!*

Developing a Language of Influence – the PANEL Method

We've now learned that words truly are of the essence, particularly when we're communicating by telephone – words paint pictures and when we don't have the visual element to express what we're communicating, we need to ensure that we're developing a language of influence to really impact customer perception.

We cannot afford to sound like a typical call centre, insurance company or front line serving customers. We need to communicate in a different language that differentiates us from our marketplace. We also need to choose our words carefully because typical business speak is full of neutrals and negatives:
"No problem,"
"no worries,"
"don't worry,"
"it shouldn't be a problem,"
"don't hesitate to give us a call if you have any further problems or issues."

The brain can't process a negative. If I told you **not** to think of a blue elephant, your brain has to picture it, right?

32

Likewise, when you say to a customer, *"no problem," "don't hesitate," "don't worry,"* etc., you should know exactly how your customer is processing that message. Negative and neutral speak, or RIP language, as we prefer to call it, is not having the desired impact on your customer's experience in terms of you sounding different from the other players out there. Typical RIP language also doesn't have the desired effect in increasing the impact of your verbal element when you're on the phone – which needs to be four times more impactful, remember!

How then, can we develop a language of influence to make the most of our verbal impact? We need to take a closer look at those dirty dozen RIP words and phrases that are used every day in call centre environments or front-line teams just like yours. Those are the words and phrases that have a negative or neutral impact on the customer and find words that increase our chances of having a bigger or better impact on our customer's experience. We do that through creating a positive alternative to neutral or negative everyday language, by applying the PANEL Method (Positive Alternatives to Neutral/Negative Everyday Language).

Here's a list of the "dirty dozen" – they're the most commonly used words and phrases in front-line operations today. Take the time to review what RIP words and phrases you are using that are not impactful in any way. Then have a go at creating a more positive alternative to saying the same thing.

The Dirty Dozen

1. **The SORRY word...**
   "Sorry to keep you waiting."
   "I'm sorry you've been on hold so long."

2. **The BUT word...**
   "I hear what you're saying, but..."
   "I know that, but..."

3. **The WORRY word...**
   "Don't worry, it shouldn't be a problem."
   "No worries!"

4. **The BEAR word...**
   "Bear with me, I won't be a second."
   "Can you just bear with me a minute?"

5. **The PROBLEM word...**
   "No problem!"
   "That's not a problem!"

6. **The TROUBLE word...**
   "The trouble is... we've got a backlog at the moment."
   "No trouble!"

34

7. The LEAVE IT word…

"Leave it with me and I'll get back to you ASAP."

"Leave it to me and I'll sort it!"

8. The HESITATE word…

"Don't hesitate to contact me if you have any queries."

"If you get any more problems, don't hesitate to call me."

9. The YOU'RE WRONG word…

"You've come through to the wrong department; I'll have to transfer you to…"

"You've pressed the wrong number; you need to re-dial to go through to Accounts…"

10. The WE'RE WRONG word…

"I'm ever so sorry but… we sent the details to your old address."

"Sorry they didn't get back to you – can I help at all?"

11. The AFRAID word…

"I'm afraid we don't deal with that here."

"The lines are all busy at the moment I'm afraid…"

12. The UNFORTUNATELY word…

"Unfortunately, the Agreement doesn't cover you for that."

"We need authorisation from the account holder unfortunately."

Spot any that you *know* you're guilty of saying?

Here are a few PANEL examples you may wish to try out for some of the R.I.P words listed here:

1. **The SORRY word...**
   "Thank you for your patience."
   "Thank you for waiting/holding the line for me."

2. **The BUT word...**
   "I can certainly appreciate that and..."
   "I do understand, although..."

3. **The WORRY word...**
   "Be assured, I'll take care of that for you."
   "My pleasure/That's fine/You're welcome."

4. **The BEAR word...**
   "Let me just check that for you."
   "Just a moment while I look into that for you."

5. **The PROBLEM word...**
   "You're welcome/Happy to help!/Certainly..."
   "I'll do that for you/I can sort that for you."

6. **The TROUBLE word...**
   "The situation is.../the position is...You're

welcome/my pleasure/glad I could help!"

7. The LEAVE IT word…
"I'll certainly look into this for you and get back to you before…/by…/within… (timeframe)."
"I'll get onto this straight away and call you with an update/some more information/an answer before…/by…/within… (timeframe)."

8. The HESITATE word…
"Feel free to contact me if you need any more information/have any more questions."
"Do get in touch/please give me a call if you require further help/support/advice about…"

9. The YOU'RE WRONG word…
"So that you're speaking to the best people who can help you, let me put you through to our Accounts department."
"In order to sort this out for you, let me give you the direct dial for our Accounts team."

10. The WE'RE WRONG word…
"On behalf of the Admin team, I apologise that we've sent the details to your old address."
"Oh, that's really surprising/unusual for (name of colleague) and I'm so sorry you've had to call back – you're speaking with (your name), may I help you?"

11. The AFRAID word... (just *drop it*!)

"I recommend you speak with (name of department) who deals with that – let me put you through."

"I can certainly take a message and ask the team to call you back, as the lines are busy at the moment."

12. **The UNFORTUNATELY word...** (just *drop it*!)

*"The Agreement **does** cover you for... although it doesn't cover you for."*

"We can certainly organise this for you, once we've had authorisation from the account holder."

Our words are the vessels on which our thoughts are created and they are the clothes our thoughts wear – so dress them well.

Giving a WIIFY (What's In It For You)

So here's a little tip designed to lead your customers or prospects to do as you ask. It's a very simple and straightforward technique that works by appealing to human nature, by letting people know "what's in it for them" **first.**

As an example, how many times do we need to put a customer on hold during our working day? And how often do we hear ourselves or others say:

"Is it okay if I put you on hold and double check that with my manager?"
or
"I'm just going to pop you on hold while I check…"
or
"can you hold the line a moment for me?"

Using a WIIFY first, listen to how different the request sounds:

"So that I'm giving you the most up-to-date information, let me double check that with my manager. Are you happy to hold while I do that?"
   or

"So that I'm giving you the correct details, let me ask my colleague about that – are you OK to hold for a moment?"

Why does it land differently? When you don't *first* give the WIIFY or the benefit of someone doing as you ask, the customer's brain immediately interprets having to do something for **you** first, before you're able to do something for **them** – and that's not great customer service is it?

As another example, if a customer has come through to the wrong department and you need to transfer them, if you use a WIIFY first, then your customer is far less likely to feel annoyed that they're being passed around the building! For example,

"So that you're speaking to the best people who can help you, let me put you through to our customer service team."

This lands much differently than saying,

"You've come through to the wrong department, I'll have to transfer you to our customer service team, who can help you."

As a final example, if you're in a financial services or compliance environment, you are well aware of your need to do a security check before you're able to help a customer, probably saying something like,

"I just need to ask you some security questions"
or
"for data-protection purposes, can you confirm your date of birth and first line of address for me?"

Using a WIIFY first, notice how differently the request sounds:

"In order for me to access your personal agreement, can you confirm...,"
or
"To protect your confidential information, please can you confirm your date of birth and first line of address for me?"

Remember, human nature dictates how a customer will behave for you. So whenever you need or want them to do **anything at all** for you, make sure you give them a WIIFY **first!**

> ***Experience is what you get when you didn't get what you wanted!***

Applying the Second Option Technique

Here's another little tip that works brilliantly when combined with the WIIFY. It's called the Second Option Technique and it is designed to help the customer feel in control, to feel as though they have a choice of what to do and therefore, help them feel more in charge.

Whenever we can offer a customer a choice of actions, where we're happy with either action they take, we create the *illusion* of choice for the customer, enhancing their sense of personal control. There are a few rules however, when using the Second Option Technique. First, two options only, both of which must be similar and acceptable to us and to our customer. Secondly, the latter option we give is the option **we** would *prefer* them to take, following the Recency Rule to influence the customer (the most recent one given will be the one they are more likely to go for). Thirdly, we change our vocal tone and inflection to encourage acceptance of that second option.

For example,

"So that I'm giving you the correct information, I'd like to double check that with my colleague. I can see if she's available at the moment, or to save you holding, I can give you a call back within the hour. What's best for you?"

In this example, we would rather the customer get off the phone, perhaps because we have calls queuing and that's why we offered that choice second and changed our vocal tone to influence their decision to accept that option. Who feels in control? Our customer does. Who's actually in control? We are!

Use the Second Option Technique whenever you have a choice of actions that your customer can take e.g. different payment methods, different ways to confirm details to us, different ways to get through to another department, different ways to set up a contract or agreement with us – and create that illusion of choice and control for your customer.

It's another 1% idea that just might make a 100% difference to how your customer feels about their experience with your company. And as we know, customers will forget what we say and do for them, but they will never forget how we make them **feel**. So help your customer to **feel** empowered, with the use of the Second Option Technique.

You can't solve a problem from the same level of consciousness at which it was created!

Following the UPOD Rule
(Under Promise, Over Deliver)

This is an easy technique you can use from your toolkit, which will help you to better manage both your customers' expectations and your own workload and stress levels. It's called the UPOD Rule and it stands for Under Promise, Over Deliver.

Despite our best intentions, most of us spend most of our time over-promising and then end up under-delivering. For example, when we tell a customer that we need to double-check something for them and we'll call them *"straight back"* or *"in five minutes"* we've immediately over-promised and put additional stress on ourselves to now go and sort things out right away!

If you're like most front liners I know, your working day is busy and chances are when you put the phone down to that customer who you've promised to reply to straight away, or watch them walk out your premises, there'll be another beep in your ear and another complex call or difficult customer that needs sorting out or another "tricky" customer walk in, so you won't be able to deliver on that promise that you've just made.

45

The next time you have to manage a customer's expectations, do yourself a big favour and under-promise so that you meet and maybe even exceed their expectations. How can you do this? Just by taking the focus away from the *time* that you're going to be doing something in and placing it on what you're *doing* for them instead.

Three little words that can help you achieve this – **by, before** and **within**.

Let me give you an example: you need to double-check something with your manager before you can help the customer, but they're in a meeting so you'll have to call the customer back. Here's how you can manage their expectation much better using the UPOD Rule. Remember to give a WIIFY first!

*"So that we can resolve this situation, I'll need to get my manager to sign this off for you, so I'll do that as soon as she's back from her meeting and get back to you **before** close of play today [or "**by** lunchtime" or "**within** the hour,"] is that okay with you, Mr Customer?"*

We then create a bit more of a window of time for ourselves to work on the customer's query or request and we stand a much better chance of responding to them within the time-frame, so we meet their expectations as a bare minimum – and maybe even exceed them.

When you say to a customer "*I'll be back to you in five minutes*" or *"straight away"*, then that's exactly when they expect you to be back to them – straight away or in five minutes!

When you say *"within the hour"* and it's 10 o'clock, they expect you to be back to them by 11 so if you call at 10:30 or 10:40 or 10:50 or even two minutes to 11, then you'll have managed their expectation.

Likewise, if we say to a customer "*I'll get back to you by close of play*", they expect you to respond between 5:00 and 5:30. So give yourself a break and take the pressure off your own time frames and manage your customers' expectations much better with the use of the UPOD Rule. And remember those three little words: **by, before** and **within**.

> *Most people would rather do a job they love for less, than do a job they hate for more*

Applying the KISS Principle
(Keep It Simple and Straightforward)

The essence of great customer service and effective communication is to Keep It Simple and Straightforward!

Don't use 20 words when 10 will do and use language that mirrors and matches the customer so that you're on the same wavelength, by talking their language.

Remember that it's important to create a natural, conversational tone when you're engaging with customers, especially on the phone, so avoid that typical "call centre" language and get rid of those R.I.P phrases!

In applying the KISS Principle, it's important too that you avoid all jargon or techie talk and speak in a way that is clear and easy to understand – remember, it's not just *what* you say, it's the *way* that you say it – *that's* what gets results!

And most vitally of all – remember that people buy (or buy into) people *first*, so being personable, polite and friendly, easy on the ear, positive in word and deed are all good ways to follow the KISS Principle. Effective communication ain't rocket science you know! As the meerkat would say *"simples!"*

> ***Absence of evidence is not evidence of absence!***

Managing Difficult Conversation (1) – the Tape Technique

Operating within a customer-service environment means there will always be times when a difficult conversation must be had with a prospect, customer or colleague.

For example, telling a customer that we can't action their request immediately because they've rung in past the cut-off time, or advising a customer that we can't change their payment date until the next due date which is a month away, or letting a customer know that they can't start their agreement with us until the first of next month.

When you face these difficult scenarios, it's completely natural to focus on the negative first, and this creates an unnecessary negative reaction, or negative impact on the other person.

There is a psychological reaction going on in the brain when we deliver what lands as "bad news" because we all have these two constantly playing tapes in our brain and the trick is to start the positive tape (the good news tape or can-do tape) playing

first, so that when you deliver that bit of bad news, it gets delivered onto the positive tape, lessening the negative impact, so that the bad news lands more positively.

Let's imagine for a moment that I'm a smoker and I pop into my local shop and ask for 20 Silk Cut and the shop assistant starts her response with,
"I'm ever so sorry but…"
or
"Unfortunately…"
or
"I'm afraid to tell you that…"
…we kind of know what's coming next, don't we?

Yes, it's going to be some bad news – they don't have my brand in stock. Although the assistant in the kiosk did start her response with some bad news, thus starting my negative tape to set play first, she did in fact go on to give me a little bit of good news, which was that she'd be happy to give me a superior brand for the same price as my cheaper brand! Not ideal, but certainly better than no cigarettes at all if you're a smoker! Yet sadly, that little bit of good news was delivered onto my negative, or bad news tape, because that was the one that was set to play *first* – make sense?

So what did that do to the good news? Well, it diluted it at best, and it perhaps even negated it altogether, at worst. We can use the Tape Technique, a clever little tip that uses reverse psychology to deliver a negative message or a bit of bad news, by setting our customers' **positive** tape to play first whenever we have a little bit of bad news to deliver.

In my cigarette scenario, the shop assistant could say something like this:

"I can certainly give you a superior brand called 'Super Superior' for the same price as a packet of Silk Cut, 20 however the delivery van hasn't turned up today, so I don't have any Silk Cut in stock. Is that okay with you?"

Notice how different that response sounds using the Tape Technique to deliver that negative message, because the positive tape was set to play first, so when the bad news was given, it was delivered onto my positive tape.

What did that do to the bad news? Well, it diluted it. It doesn't make it go away – we still have to tell the customer that we can't do what they're asking - but the bad news lands much more pleasantly to the ear, than if we were to start that negative tape rolling first.

It's a brilliant little technique that works as well in home life as it does in business. For example, if your child asks if their friend can come to tea tomorrow, but you're working late and won't even be home to cook your **own** son's tea, then you can deliver that bit of bad news in a way that keeps their mood high and your guilt low, using the Tape Technique.

Here's how:

"Yes, of course Johnny can come to tea, and maybe you can even have a sleepover, and we'll have to do it on Friday, as Mummy's at work until 8 o'clock tomorrow. Is that alright darling?"

Do you have any specific scenarios in your day-to-day conversations with customers or colleagues, where you need to deliver a little bit of "bad news"?

Take a moment now to try using a positive alternative by applying the Tape Technique to that difficult conversation – focus first on what you *can* do, before focusing on what you can't! Tell your customer some good news, before you tell them the bad! Discuss the positives before you discuss the negatives! Try saying *yes* to something before you have to say *no*!

> ***Our thoughts are our greatest allies, but they can be our most powerful enemies too!***

Managing Difficult Conversation (2) – The FPQ Technique

When there's a bit of bad news to give to a customer or prospect but there's a little bit of good news to tell, then nothing is more powerful than the Tape Technique. However, what if we have *no* good news at all to give to a customer or prospect? I'm sure we've all been in that difficult position where we've had to tell a customer that the answer is no, that we can't do what they're asking? For example, their agreement with us doesn't allow us to take that action or we can't help them any further because they've not complied with the terms and conditions of their contract. It's at times like this when we subconsciously or even unconsciously find ways to soften the blow, usually with apologetic language like

"I'm ever so sorry, but that's not covered under your agreement,"

or

"Unfortunately we don't offer refunds under those terms."

Usually, we'll unconsciously change our vocal tone and inflection, even lower the volume or pitch and maybe speed up a little, almost as if we're struggling to utter the words from our throat! Once we give the negative reply, we sit with baited breath hoping the customer will empathise with the difficult situation we're in.

What we fail to recognise is that there is something very real happening when we're faced with the difficult situation of having to tell a customer we can't help them – both physiologically and psychologically. No matter how difficult or rude or obnoxious the customer may be in these awkward scenarios, it doesn't *feel* good and **we** don't feel good when we know we can't help someone, because of course, that's our job – to help and serve our customers!

We chose to work within a customer-service environment because we enjoy serving others. We like to provide a service, we like to help people. So when we can't do our job properly, all sorts of reactions start to kick off both inside and outside of us. We may become a bit hot or flustered or croaky-sounding or fidget a little or stumble over our words.

When we're in a position like this, feeling stressed and anxious about what we're having to tell someone, our logical, rational brain has quite literally shut down and the limbic brain has taken over. This is the part of the brain that houses our fight-or-flight response and where there are unwelcomed endorphins, our amygdala, either side of the brain, hijacking our reasoning and our logic.

Unless and until we calm those alarm bells, the amygdala will ensure nothing positive or assertive or rational will come out of our mouths. Now the good news is there are several ways to sort the amygdala hijack, to re-awaken the neo-cortex part of our brain and ensure our verbal and vocal all-bad-news message is delivered in a logical, factual, rational way, while maintaining rapport with the other person.

There are physical strategies (pinch yourself hard, squeeze your toes in your shoes, dig a pen into your palm) and there are mental strategies that can awaken the rational part of the brain (counting backwards from 100 to 3 in threes for example). Then there are verbal strategies which will enable you to deliver that bad news to your customer or prospect in an empathetic yet totally assertive way.

Our best verbal strategy to share with you is known as the FPQ Technique. We first verbally express how *we* are **feeling** about this difficult situation, before we explain the **position** we are in, then asking a **question** to test for acceptance or agreement to the situation.

Let's have a look at the FPQ Technique in practice. I'm sure those of you that work within the financial services industry will relate to the scenario in which we have to tell a customer they must settle late payment charges or accept there will be no further refunds or even that we're not able to extend their payment arrangements any further.

We can probably all relate to the usual response we'd give to these situations – we either find ourselves defending our corner, ready to fight as opposed to flee, perhaps even sounding a little curt as we tell a customer they've broken the rules so it's their fault they're now in this position! Or we plan to take flight by stumbling over our words, being apologetic or sounding weak. However, when we apply the FPQ Technique and think about how we deliver the message too, by using our vocal tone and inflection to inject sincerity into our voice, the response can be much more effective. For example:

"I feel so upset and frustrated that we find ourselves in this position with your agreement. It's my job to help you and keep your account up-to-date because as responsible lenders, that's what we're here to do for you, as our customer (**feeling**).

However, we're now in the third month of non-payment on the account and the terms and conditions of your agreement do state clearly that this breech will result in closure of the account unless you're able to bring your agreement fully up-to-date which you've explained you're unable to do. (**position**)

So can you appreciate why we're having to do this?/Does that all make sense and have I explained myself well enough? (**question**)

You are much more likely to win your customer to your side when you verbally express how *you are feeling* about the situation. It's almost a mind game you're playing, looking to create some empathy from your customer so they appreciate it's not personal and you are just doing your job.

I've often heard those very words when I've been coaching at desk with clients and they've used the FPQ Technique to deliver an all bad-news message. Many times I've heard responses such as:

"Look, I know it's not your fault…"
"I know you're just doing your job…"
"I'm not having a go at you…"
"I know it's not personal…"
"I'm sure if it were down to you, you'd sort it out for me"

That's the best response you can hope for when you're in a difficult position like this one, where you have to tell a customer you can't do your job properly because you can't help them.

Consider your most frequent difficult scenarios where you have *no* good news at all to share with a customer and create your response using the FPQ Technique, so that you have some practical ideas at the ready if and when you have to tell a customer *no*!

Remember, this technique is all about "shooting from the hip" in an assertive yet totally empathetic way, so that you're able to maintain rapport with your customer, despite having to give them bad news – and **rapport** is the Golden Thread of effective communication you know!

> *Don't lower your goals to the level of your abilities. Instead, raise your abilities to the height of your goals!*

Managing Difficult Conversation (3) – The ABC Technique

How often do you face that difficult situation with a customer or prospect where you're just going around in circles with the conversation? How often does it feel like you're speaking a different language to your customer or they appear to be living on a different planet because you can't seem to make them understand what you're explaining?

It can be frustrating, particularly so if you work in a busy call centre environment where calls are waiting on your wallboard and you're desperately trying to wrap up the conversation, so you can continue with your working day. Or you have other customers waiting in a queue to talk to you, and that one customer or prospect is hogging all the limelight!

A great little 1% idea you can use to bring that conversation to a close in a way that is assertive yet maintains rapport with your customer is to use the ABC Technique. It stands for Assertive Boundary Control.

The ideal format for use of ABC, though you don't have to use these words, is…

"I understand...."
"Although...."
"Therefore...."

The format is designed to first give empathy and understanding to the customer's situation, then to assert some authority on the position you and they are in, then to put the ball firmly in the other person's court with the action they're required to take in order to move things forward.

Example:

*"**I understand** you're really frustrated and angry about the situation, **although**, as I've explained, I can't authorise your request until we've received written confirmation from your bank. **Therefore**, can I recommend that you call them again and ask them to email you the consent form, so we can move things forward for you, is that okay with you?"*

Are there any particular scenarios that you face in which you need to push back assertively and call time on a conversation while maintaining rapport to ensure a positive, memorable experience for your customer? If so, try using the ABC Technique to call that 'round-in-circles' conversation to a close next time.

> *To have what we've never had, we must do what we've never done!*

Managing Difficult Conversation (4) – The Reframe Technique

Here's another little one-percenter designed to help you manage a difficult conversation. How many times do you have to prove a customer wrong? How often do you hear a customer spout the terms and conditions at you, thinking they know more about your products and services than you do? Do you ever have to tell a customer they haven't got their facts straight?

These types of customers tend to bring out the worst in us. We almost want them to lose face and look stupid for being in the wrong, while making ourselves feel a little smug. knowing we have the facts right and we know better, agree?

It's so important that we keep rapport intact when we need to tell a customer they're factually incorrect in what they're saying and the way to do this is through this fabulous little tip – the Reframe Technique.

First, we find something to **agree** on, so that our customer or prospect feels a sense of one-upmanship or satisfaction that they've been proven right. They're then on the back foot when we then **disagree** with what they've said. The Reframe Technique serves two powerful purposes. First, it helps the other person save face and not look stupid when they discover they have their facts wrong and secondly, it ensures the rapport you've built during the conversation remains fully intact.

Here's a real case scenario a client of ours faces almost every day when their customer calls to complain about too much money being taken from their account on the final direct debit of their car loan agreement, after which the car is rightfully owned by them. Part of this final payment includes what's known as an "option to purchase fee". All car loan companies have this fee applied at the end of the agreement and it's taken right at the end of the term to transfer ownership and remove all interest in the car by the finance provider.

This option to purchase fee is made very clear at the start of the agreement and it's also very clearly explained in the terms and conditions of the contract, that the customer doesn't become the rightful owner of the car until the option to purchase fee is settled at the end of the contract as part of the final payment.

The conversation usually involves the customer kicking off about so-called "hidden charges" and this fee not being explained at the outset and sometimes even demanding to remove the charge because they feel they've been wrongly informed. It's all too tempting to climb on our high horse in this situation, especially when we have the proof that the customer is wrong and we are right.

But fuelling the fire only creates a furnace and it's definitely not the way to win an argument with a customer! So using the Reframe Technique, we might say instead:

"I agree with you, Mr Customer. It's extremely frustrating when you think you've settled an agreement, only to discover there's a final fee to pay, although I disagree that the option to purchase fee is something that was hidden from you, as it clearly states in your contract that the fee is payable as part of the final payment in order to rightfully transfer ownership of the car to you. I'm very happy to email you a copy of the contract that you signed so that you can be assured it is a condition of the loan if you'd like me to?"

Or we might say:

"I agree, Mr Customer, it is an odd term to refer to it as an 'option to purchase fee', because there isn't actually an option not to pay the fee, as it is the only way the car becomes rightfully yours and we release any claims on it as your finance provider. I disagree, however, that the way the fee works wasn't explained

to you at the start of your contract, because on page four of the agreement that you signed, it does clearly set out what the option to purchase fee is, how much it is, and when it will be taken from you. I can certainly send you a copy of your signed agreement if that would help clarify things for you?"

A few key points to remember to ensure that you use the Reframe Technique to best effect: First, the words "*I agree that*" followed by "*I disagree that*" are crucial. When a customer hears first, "*I agree with you*" their guard comes down and they feel more receptive to whatever else you have to say, so that when you say, "*I disagree, however*" this message lands much better on the ear. Secondly, when you tell the customer they're wrong, you must bring on the evidence that proves that. In this example, the proof is the actual wording in the finance agreement.

Are there any particular scenarios that **you** face where you need to prove a customer wrong and put them straight while maintaining rapport and helping them save face? If so, have a go at creating some reframe responses that you can refer to if and when you face those difficult conversations with your customers or prospects in the future.

> *You can't hire other people to do your push ups for you!*

Vocal Power –
the Key Ingredients of Vocal Communication

When we think about the impact of our vocal communication face-to-face, it comes as no surprise that it has over five times more impact than the verbal element of our communication. You may remember from a previous chapter that our vocal factor represents 38% of the impact that our communication has on another person when we're engaging with them for the very first time, yet our verbal factor represents just 7% of the impact.

Many of you reading this book will be engaging with customers for the first time many times a day over a telephone, rather than face-to-face and if that's you, then remember that our vocal factor plays an even more important role, because our sound and the quality of our voice needs to make up for what we've lost with the absence of our visual communication.

In Mehrabian's Model, our vocal factor represents 70% of the impact and our verbal factor accounts for 30% when we're engaging with others over the phone.

So we need to work hard to improve the *quality of our sound* when we're engaging with our customers and prospects over the phone, in order to create a better, bigger impact on their experience of us. How do we do this?

There is a school of thought that says your voice is just your voice and unless you put on some kind of telephone voice, which will simply make you sound false or unnatural, then there isn't very much you can do about the sound of your voice.

We certainly wouldn't advocate that you put on some kind of special voice or try changing your accent to try and have a greater impact on your customers or prospects because of course, your sound is part of you, and that includes your accent, although you ought to be aware that some accents are harder to understand – and good vocal sound is all about clarity.

If you do have an accent that isn't quite so pleasing to the ear, just be aware of the need to be clear with the other elements that make up your vocal factor and work a little harder to ensure that those elements have more impact on your customer's experience.

Our vocal communication is made up of several elements including:

69

- our **tone of voice**, which Mehrabian referred to as the "mood of the voice", being a direct reflection of our mood within.

- our **pitch** and whether it's high or low.

- our **inflection** which is the rise and fall of the voice, sometimes referred to as the "rhythm" of the voice.

- our **pace** or **speed** of sound, linked very closely to our **pausing rate** and how well we pace and pause for clarity and effect.

- our **volume** – how loudly or softly we speak.

- our **clarity** of sound, which is linked very closely to all these elements *and* our accent too.

A word about tone, or the "mood of the voice": If you work on a phone, then the one sure place that your customer or prospect will hear what kind of attitude you have towards them and their enquiry or query and how interested or committed or customer-focused you sound, will be in those critical first 4 to 14 seconds when you answer the call. Not on *what* you say, but in *how* you say it – your tone and rhythm of voice as you welcome your caller onto the line.

Can you recall a time when something funny happened in the office or someone had just told a joke as you answered a call? Notice how upbeat and positive and enthusiastic your tone of voice sounded because your mood is exactly that, at that moment. Remember that you can have a positive impact on the person at the other end of the phone right from the outset.

And of course, the opposite can happen too, can't it? If you've just clicked off from a very difficult call or caller who's been very rude or aggressive with you and you've not had time to rid your mind of those negative thoughts and feelings that you have about that call or caller, notice how your tone of voice sounds when you welcome the next caller onto the line?

Our customers want to engage with someone who sounds as though they're enjoying what they're doing and we owe it to our customers to answer the phone in a good mood. So ensure that your mood of voice is a good one each and every time you make or take a call, whether that's your first or one hundredth call of the day.

Focus on some of those in-the-moment attitude builders that we've looked at in an earlier chapter, in order to ensure you *sound* upbeat and positive – like checking your posture, breathing purposefully, strolling for a blast of fresh air, or walking to the end of the office and back again, or drinking a glass of room temperature water, or eating a square of good quality chocolate, or a piece of fruit, or standing up and having a stretch. Do anything that will ensure you adopt the right state, so that you answer the phone in the right mood, because that will come across loud and clear in your vocal tone as you welcome your callers onto the line.

And of course, this applies equally to the tone of our voice when we're face to face with our customers too!

We owe it to everyone that we speak with to meet and greet them in a positive, upbeat and customer-focused manner that sets the right **tone** for the rest of the call or conversation.

A word about inflection: It's a big part of our tone of voice. If we think about our tone being the overall mood of the voice, then inflection is the rise and fall, or rhythm of the voice. When we have good inflection it serves two very powerful purposes. First, it makes us interesting to listen to - and it's as important to be *interesting*, than it is to be *interested*!

Secondly, it enables us to give more emphasis or more impact to particular parts of our conversation, by stressing certain words or phrases, so that we influence our customer's acceptance of what we're saying or suggesting.

For example, whichever word I stress in this sentence will control the meaning understood by its audience.

"*I* didn't say she stole the money."
"I *didn't* say she stole the money."
"I didn't *say* she stole the money."
"I didn't say *she* stole the money."
"I didn't say she *stole* the money."
"I didn't say she stole *the* money."
"I didn't say she stole the *money*."

A "quick" word about pace: This is another little one-percenter of the vocal element where we can create better impact, if we s—l—o—w down. There is an ideal rate at which you and I should be communicating for good impact (especially when on the phone) and that is a rate of between 140 and 160 words per minute. You can try out the Rate of Speech exercise in this chapter, to test how close to the ideal rate you are! Get someone to time you – be yourself, read out the passage as if you were having a conversation with someone and see how on target you are (it should take between 140 and 160 seconds

73

to read out those 160 words at a pace that is ideal for communicating effectively!)

> *Inspiration comes from perspiration!*

Vocal Communication:
Rate Of Speech Exercise

"As a representative of your Company on the telephone, it is important that you speak clearly. This means you must speak so that you can be understood.

"Although there is no set rate of speech, most expert speakers talk at between one hundred and forty and one hundred and sixty words per minute, as I am now.

"This is a good speed for telephone communication. It is not too fast to be understood and it does not give the impression that you are under pressure. Nor is it too slow.

"The one hundred and sixty-word rate adds an element of dignity to your voice.

"The one hundred and sixty-word rate also gives a sound image to the caller that establishes both you and your Company as efficient and well organised.

"To give the listener the kind of impression of yourself and your Company that you wish, speak correctly; speak at one hundred and sixty."

Two quick fixes to slowing down and managing the volume button as well, is to check out your posture and practise proper breathing technique. If you're dealing with a tricky customer or someone kicking off, then we tend to increase our speed or pace, and either increase or decrease the volume, and this is mainly due to our breathing technique having gone a little awry. Sit up straight and forward, or if you're on the 'phone, even stand up so that psychologically you are looking down on the other person and you'll feel more in control and more confident.

Take a few deep, but quiet breaths through your nose, while letting your tummy muscles go, and then breathe out through your mouth while holding your tummy muscles in. That will help you better control your pace and volume. It'll improve the quality of your voice, because the voice is just a set of muscles that requires exercise to be fit and healthy just like any other muscle in our body. Good posture and good breathing technique will help you do this, and it will ensure that your vocal communication has a bigger impact overall on your customer's experience.

A final word about **vocal** communication. It's a health and safety warning about protecting your voice to ensure that your vocal sound is of good quality and impactful when you're speaking to customers and prospects throughout the day. Ensure those vocal cords are well-watered with room-temperature drinking water, not fizz or ice-cold drinks because they tend to constrict the vocal cords and ensure that you're exercising the voice properly through correct breathing, through the right posture and through a few mouth movements and sounds to warm up first thing in the morning or at the start of your shift. You only have one voice but there are several elements to it – and several ways to make the most of it when you're engaging with customers, *especially* over the phone. Make the most of those vocal factors and remember **clarity** is key!

> *Dreams come in a size too big so we can grow into them!*

Questioning Skills and Probing Techniques

The real skill of effective questioning is in our ability to create conversation, rather than interrogation! In this chapter, we'll take a look at a few 1% ideas that will ensure we create a 100% conversational tone to the **find out** stage, so that we sound natural, unscripted and genuinely interested in our customer's answers to our questions.

First, let's take a little revisit of the basics; we all know about **open** and **closed** questions, and their purpose and power in the find-out stage of a call or conversation, at least in theory, correct?

If you went to the same training school as I did, then you'd have been taught that you ask *open questions* at the opening of the conversation, to open up the customer or prospect, to get more detailed information, a more expansive response, or detailed answer – and you ask *closed questions* at the close of the conversation, to gain commitment and test for agreement.

You may also have learned the little model I was given to help me remember how open questions begin. I was taught the rugby-post model, with the H as the goal-post standing for **How** and then all the W questions along the goal bar, which represented the rugby players' bottoms, i.e. **what, why, when, where, who** and **which!**

All the theory around basic probing skills is fine, although as you and I know, what really matters is what works in practice. One of the most commonly-asked questions can be asked either open-ended, *"How are you?"* or closed, *"Are you okay?"*

Both are the same question, but not necessarily getting you an answer that's by the book! For example, *"How are you?"* might evoke a *"fine thanks,"* response, which is short and exact. Whereas *"Are you okay?"* may elicit a very expansive, detailed response, that only an open question is supposed to get you. For example:

"Well, actually, Marie, no, I'm not, now you've asked. You see, the other day, I was talking to David, and he reminded me that I've done almost 20 hours overtime this month, and I'm feeling really exhausted, and I'm not sure how long I can go on like this ..."

You get the picture! So here's a clever little one-percenter that combines the power of the closed question (to deliver you very specific information), with the power of the open question (which is to yield you a very broad, expansive response), as well as ensure that conversational tone.

It's called the **Defining Question**, and it can be pre-framed with an open or closed question, because what matters is the **defining word** that we use in the question.

Here's how it works: when I first started my career, working in telemarketing, my trainer told me that I should never ask a question to which I didn't know the answer. I remember thinking at the time, *"How on earth am I going to know what every prospect is going to answer? Their businesses and staff will all be different."* It wasn't until I became a trainer myself that I fully understood what my trainer meant: decide on the *answer* you need, and *then* design your *question.*

Using a defining word will encourage your customer to answer in a way that you've subliminally suggested. For example, asking someone *"what has happened?"* is a good open question, but turning it into a defining question helps you get to the root of the situation much quicker and slicker.

For example *"Tell me, is there a **specific** reason for this happening?"*
(this is a Closed Defining Question)

*"When, **precisely** did this happen?"*
or
*"what **exactly** has happened?*
(these latter two are Open Defining Questions).

Other defining words that can be added to the open or closed question include:

- **exact/exactly**
- **specific/specifically**
- **precise/precisely**
- **in particular/particularly**
- **actual/actually**
- **briefly**
- **realistically**
- **normally**
- **in general/generally**
- **usual/usually**
- **briefly…..**

Here's your next little one-percenter for effective **questioning**: it's that very powerful, yet highly interrogational, potentially accusatory question – **WHY?** It's an important open question, particularly if a customer hasn't done something they should have, like settled their monthly account or telephoned in sooner with their problem.

It's a good question and we just need to find a way to soften it a little, so that we don't cause any defensiveness in our customer. The easiest way to do that is to pre-frame the why question with a:

"M*ay I ask...*"

or an

"Out of interest..."

...remembering to change your vocal tone and inflection and lower the volume as you ask the "why" question.

For example:

"May I ask why you're only phoning in about this now?"

or

"And out of interest, why is that?"

The next little one-percenter I want to share with you regarding effective questioning is the **Conditional Question**. It's traditionally used in sales to negotiate a win-win outcome, but equally powerful in customer-service land, when we need to reach an agreement with our customer or prospect. The trick to using this questioning technique well is to ensure that you frame the question to "condition" the customer to comply with your terms.

All too often, we let the customer know what we're going to do for them first, and we lose our ability to influence them. So we might say,

"I'll waive the late payment fee for you if you're able to settle your account and bring your payments up-

to-date by the end of this week. Is that okay with you?"

A more effective use of the Conditional Question is to let them know what you are going to do for them *after* they have done something for you. This little tip follows the same principle as the Second Option Technique that we looked at in an earlier chapter, where the Recency Rule applies, meaning the customer will remember the last thing you said, when both statements are deemed as good news, or acceptable to them. For example:

"If you're able to get the signed contracts back to me within the next working week, then I'll hold the special offer price for you – how does that sound to you?"

The question that's asked at the end of the condition should always be a **True Response Question** or TRQ. That is, any question that gives your customer an opportunity to answer you truthfully, without feeling tied-down or pushed into a corner, like so many of those closing sales questions tend to do:

"You are okay with that, aren't you?"
"If you're happy with that, I'll go ahead and set that up for you, shall I?"
"So that's alright, isn't it?"

Examples of TRQs may include:

"How does that sound to you?"
"Are you happy with that?"
"Does that all make sense to you?"
"Have I explained that well enough?"
"Is that acceptable to you?"

We want our customer to tell us the truth at this point. We don't want them to go away not feeling committed, or clear about what they need to do to take action. The True Response Question ensures that if there is any misunderstanding, or something's not clear, then we deal with it there and then.

My penultimate little one-percenter to share with you on effective questioning is the very well-researched and proven strategy of the **Power of Three**, particularly if you're in an environment where you do need to ask a lot of questions.

So ask your questions in sets of three and then do a little summary, or confirm, or verbal signpost into the next set of three questions. The find-out stage becomes much more conversational and free-flowing when you use the Power of Three and will feel much less like an interrogation or an interview!

What's the proof? Well, it's how our brains have learned and adopted knowledge since we were children. We all learned our A-B-C; our 1-2-3; there's the good, the bad and the ugly; three blind mice; we know every story has a beginning, a middle and an end; there's see no evil, hear no evil, speak no evil and of course, we all know the old saying that bad luck comes in threes!

Branding gurus know more about the Power of Three to market their products and services than anyone else on the planet: "*A Mars a day helps you work, rest, and play*"; "*Every little helps*"; "*Making life better*"; "*Snap, crackle and pop*"; "*Just Do It*"... the list is endless! The number three sits very comfortably in the brain and therefore, if you have a lot of questions to ask your prospect or customer, then make sure you ask them in sets of three.

My final little one-percenter is the reminder of the TED Principle – which works well as a pre-framer, particularly to an open question. Pre-framing your questions with;
"**T**ell me…"
or
"**E**xplain…"
or
"**D**escribe…"
…hence the TED Principle will ensure a conversational tone to the find-out stage and enables the conversation to flow more naturally and easily.

It's never too late to be who you might have been!

Active Listening –
the Fourth Communication Skill

Let's look now at what is arguably the most vital communication skill of all: **Active Listening**. It's one of the four key communication skills, yet it's the one that receives the least attention in our formal education. We were all taught how to read, write and speak properly, yet how many of us were actually *taught* how to listen?

If your education was anything like mine, then you were taught by being *told* to be quiet, get to the back of the class and pay attention to what the teacher was saying!

So it should come as no surprise that listening is not a passive skill, it's one that requires active hard work. We have to consciously and constantly work on developing and honing our listening ability in order to become an effective communicator.

As communications expert Peter Thomson taught us, "the greatest communicators are those with the greatest listening skills." and everyone needs a good listening to from time to time, especially our prospects and customers – because of course, they love nothing more than talking about themselves!

We must recognise and accept the three levels of listening in which humans operate and work damn hard to ensure that we stay in level three mode with those we want to influence.

We'll take a look at the three levels in a moment, but let's first remind ourselves of some of the key learning points around active listening. First, because it's not a passive skill, it doesn't happen naturally, unlike the other three inate communication skills. We have two ears and one mouth, and we should be using them in that ratio – listen twice as much as we are talking and in that order too.

Next, there is a substantial difference between listening and hearing. We need to be fully aware of this, especially when we work in an environment where we receive very similar types of calls or conversations and/or callers phoning in or who we need to phone out to. It's very easy to make assumptions and not pay full attention when we're hearing the same sort of thing day in and day out.

Level one listening, or unconscious listening or "yeah, yeah, yeah" mode, is a level we cannot afford to be in when we're representing our brand on the front line. This is where we are simply waiting for our turn to speak! We're just hearing sounds vibrating the ear drum and we are neither tuned in nor turned on to what our prospect or customer is saying to us.

Level two listening is subconscious listening, or ebb-and-flow listening, when we focus more on the words that are being spoken, so there'll be certain words that catch our attention and refocus us on the other person and then we'll ebb away again if our customer stops talking about something that's familiar to us.

In their book, *Why Men Don't Listen and Women Can't Read Maps*, communication psychologists Barbara and Allan Pease talk about men's inability to listen holistically. That is, in level three mode, where they are focused 100% on the other person and what they're saying and listening between the lines to the *way* things are being said, as well as what's not being said, to fully understand what the other person is communicating before responding. The authors claim that generically speaking, the part of the male brain that controls their ability to listen in level three mode is less developed than in the female brain and consequently, men tend to operate in selective listening mode!

Getting and staying in level three mode requires giving 100% of your time, attention, energy and focus on the other person. It's about putting aside your own thoughts, opinions, views and reactions and paying the other person the greatest compliment of all time. John Dewey, the renowned American philosopher and educational reformer claimed that the greatest compliment that you can pay another human being is to give that person your undivided attention and time – and that's exactly what you do when you truly, actively listen to someone.

There are 10 commandments to active listening that must be followed if we're going to enhance our relationships with others and ensure that PME – that Positive Memorable Experience for people, each and every time we interact with them.

The 10 commandments of **Level Three Listening** are:

1. **Stop talking.** You cannot truly listen to someone if you are talking over them or interrupting them.

2. **Concentrate**. Always be prepared to listen before the need arises. Use the mental enema technique – put on those listening blinkers and stay focused.

3. **Acknowledge and empathise with your customer**. Prove that you are listening and

interested by using encouraging mouth noises and giving empathy where appropriate. Sometimes words aren't even necessary. Just a tilt of the head, or a gentle nod or a smile is sufficient, even when you are listening on the telephone.

4. **Be objective**. Keep an open mind. Everyone is different and so is their reaction to any situation. So never assume.

5. **Ask questions**. Questions demand answers and therefore develop our understanding of the message. However, ensure that your questioning is conversational, not interrogational.

6. **Confirm and clarify, summarise and reflect back key words**. This is even more important if we can't see the person that we are communicating with. Reflect back key words to confirm that you've listened, that you've understood and to highlight important information and so maintain control of the situation (and remember the tip we discussed before about presenting information or questions in groups of three.) Your customer will understand that you have understood and therefore subconsciously appreciate you and what you are doing for them.

7. **Be patient**. Allow the speaker his or her say. Listen to understand, rather than to reply. Do not interrupt. Remember, listening is not about waiting for your turn to speak!

8. **Take notes.** Write the key points down on paper, or on screen. However, be careful not to put too much down on paper otherwise you'll be into "pencil listening" and vital information may be missed.

9. **Look and listen between the lines**. Look and listen for the feelings, the ideas and the meaning behind the words that are being spoken. What is *not* said, or the *way* something is said, is often just as important as what is being said.

10. **Stop talking.** It's the first and last commandment because all other commandments depend on it. Remember, we have two ears and only one mouth, so they should be used in that order and by that ratio.

Our listening skills are often put to the test with that ridiculous game of Chinese Whispers! Yet in this game, we're not allowed to ask any questions, or take any notes or ask for confirmation or clarification of anything that's been said – all those important commandments we said we need to follow in order to hone our listening skills.

So here's a much more practical exercise to put your listening skills to the test. Get someone to read the following statement out to you. As they do, ensure you use as many of the 10 commandments as possible – get the salient points down on paper; ask questions; ask for confirmation or clarification, in order to prove your understanding of what's being said. After your colleague has given you the information, they'll ask you seven straightforward questions, to which you'll write the answers down on a piece of paper. Understood? Let's begin;

Statement

Please ask your representative Chris Williams to meet John Brown from our Head Office at the bank at 12:30. Mrs. Bailey from Quality Solutions will be waiting for them in the Manager's office. Ask Chris to bring Mr. Brown and Mrs. Bailey to our showroom at 32 Bishop's Close for a meeting at 2:30. After *this* meeting, Mr. Smith will decide whether to hold any further talks on the product launch.

Here are the seven questions that your colleague should ask you once they've read out the statement to you and you've taken advantage of those 10 commandments, to develop your understanding of the message they've given you – no cheating now!

1. Who is going to the bank to meet someone?

2. What company does Mr. Brown work for?

3. What's the address of Quality Solutions?

4. Is there enough time to get to the meeting?

5. What time does the meeting begin?

6. Who is the most senior person mentioned?

7. What is the purpose of the meeting?

The correct answers are:

1. Chris Williams was going to the bank. Others were already there but dock half a point if you assumed that Chris was a man, because you broke commandment no. 4 (you made an assumption!).

2. Mr Brown's company was only ever referred to as "our Head Office". So, no points if you assumed that the company was Quality

Solutions (another assumption, as this was the only company name mentioned).

3. The address was not 32 Bishop's Close – that was the address of the showroom. The address of Quality Solutions was never given (another assumption made possibly?).

4. It depends how far away the showroom is from the bank. It might be a safe assumption that two hours is enough time, but we've still broken that commandment – we've assumed! We haven't kept an open mind, so no points if you have said that two hours is enough time!

5. 2:30 is the correct answer. There was only ever one meeting, although they were meeting **at** the bank at 12:30 to go to the actual meeting at 2:30.

6. Who knows who the most senior person mentioned is? We know nothing about their seniority or position in each of the companies. All we know are their names. We may have assumed that Mr. Smith was the most senior, because he was making decisions about a product launch. Yet marketing departments do that all the time and they're rarely the most senior person in

the whole organisation, so the answer is – we don't know!

7. We don't know the purpose of that meeting, we only know what was going to happen **after** the meeting. We don't even know whether Mr. Smith was going to be involved in that meeting. That would be something that we would want to clarify when we're being given this information.

So how did you do? Did you make a few assumptions, as we all do, most of the time and if so, what's the moral of this chapter?

Listening is about understanding not waiting for your turn to speak, so ask lots of questions; clarify and confirm understanding; never assume, even if your customer's situation is the same as the last 3 three customers that you've spoken to today, they are all different – and so their reactions to similar situations will be different.

And of course, keep in your conscious mind and in your subconscious that the greatest compliment that you can pay another human being is to give them your 100% undivided attention, time, energy and focus. So, go on, give someone a good old listening to right now and help them to feel good to have interacted with you today!

> *Challenges and obstacles are sent to instruct not obstruct – so ask yourself the question "what lesson is there for me to learn?*

Rapport –
the Golden Thread of Communication

I want to look now at what is often referred to as the Golden Thread of effective communication to encourage the win-win, in both business and in life.

It's the skill of **rapport**. And rapport is one of those words, a little bit like empathy that's used a lot in customer-service land, where we're told we must ensure rapport with our prospects and customers, because people buy people *first.* We like people who are like us, or who at least appear like us or understand us or seem like they're on the same wavelength as us.

But what does rapport mean and how do we achieve it? *The Oxford English Dictionary* defines rapport as a close and harmonious relationship in which the people concerned understand each other's feelings or ideas and communicate well.

How do we understand our customers' feelings or ideas? Well, we need to understand *them,* we need to try on *their* model of the world, get on *their* wavelength, and ask questions to understand what *they're* all about. We need to show an interest in what they're saying, listen in an active, focused way, acknowledge their responses to our questions with verbal nods, and engage in a way that pulls them in and helps them feel good, understood, and valued.

Remembering, of course, that 84% of your customers' experience is based on emotion – how they feel about their interaction with you and it's worth remembering that emotions (feelings) are processed 24 times faster than logic (facts) so spending time "up front" helping customers to "feel good" before telling them how you can help them is time well spent.

We've all spoken with prospects and customers with whom a rapport develops very naturally. We hit it off or we immediately sense that we're on the same page or we're talking the same language. The connection just feels good and right, from the outset. We all have lifelong friendships too, I'm sure, where again, we wouldn't be able to quite put our finger on it, but right from the moment we met, we just clicked.

This chapter isn't for those relationships that we happen to come across in our daily work life, where we build instant rapport and the connection feels easy and comfortable with the customer or prospect straight off. They're the easy to deal with customers or prospects! No, this chapter is for those relationships that we have to maintain or build or foster, where rapport *doesn't* come so easily or naturally, or we feel a disconnect. How do we build rapport with *these* customers or prospects?

We have to make a conscious effort to pull these types of people to us, to move closer to them, to give more of ourselves, to let more go or ignore more, to put in more effort or time, because it's our responsibility to flex our personal style or approach, or our way of communicating, in order to get that person on our side. It's not our customers' responsibility to do that – it's ours!

Remember, the definition of rapport ends with "… and they communicate well with each other." Well, the meaning of the communication is the response you receive, so if you're not getting from your customer what you want and need to reach the win-win i.e. getting them on your side, thinking alike and on the same page, then it is actually all your fault! It's a different way of looking at "the customer is always right" motto in a more realistic and practical way, in my opinion. The customer is not always right, but it is *always* your responsibility to communicate with them in a way that builds and maintains rapport, so that when they are in the wrong, and you use some of these practical one-percent tips and ideas shared here in this book, to tell them they're wrong, you're able to maintain the relationship because the Golden Thread is still running strong through your communication with them.

Onto some practical how-to's. How do we establish and keep rapport with our customers and prospects, when it hasn't happened naturally? One of the most powerful tips for building and maintaining rapport (although beware, it can also disable rapport in a nano-second) is the use of the person's name.

We all know that it can be a great controlling technique, especially when we're trying to shut a customer up by waiting for their half-a-breath and then interjecting with their name to catch their attention. However, it's also a great way to build rapport. Even if we don't like our name, get it wrong, and you will soon know about it. (Try calling me Maria or Mary if you want a sure-fire way to break rapport with me!) Of course, overuse of the person's name, or not using it at all, or only ever referring to the person as "sir" or "madam" can be an instant rapport-destroyer too.

Learning to build rapport in a natural, practical way (especially when we're engaging with customers or prospects over the phone and we've lost our visual element to influence the connection) takes time and effort. Remember, you win and influence people through a sense of knowing, liking and trusting each other – so try on other people's models of the world

101

if you want to get on-side with them. Build that relationship by talking the other person's language and mirroring and matching them on a visual, verbal and vocal level, to ensure that you arrive at that win-win destination. People buy people first, after all.

There are 10 vital steps to building rapport, which are as follows:

1. Smile – it's an outward sign of inner enthusiasm. Ensure that your internal world is positive, upbeat and optimistic in order to reflect the right attitude in your external world, because we like engaging with people who look and sound happy and positive!

2. Address the person by name after offering your name – check pronunciation, spelling and how they wish to be addressed – in order to encourage a personal connection.

3. Be genuinely interested in the other person – pick up on any comments that may encourage a more personal connection.

4. Be aware of personal space – respect other peoples' 18-inch bubble, both on *and* off the phone.

5. Ask questions – to develop your under-

standing of the other person and their situation/needs/requirements and ensure questioning is conversational, not interrogational by using open and defining questions that invite feedback.

6. Listen! Listen! Listen! Be seen and heard to listen and let others have their say, without interrupting them. Remember active, focused listening is about appreciating other peoples' model of the world. Backtrack at regular intervals by reflecting back key words and phrases to prove you have understood and to maintain trust.

7. Mirror and match the other person – learn to use mirroring and matching techniques through your visual, verbal and vocal communication in order to deepen the rapport. We like people who are like us or who we feel we're engaged with.

8. Be conscious of your own communication – visual (body language), verbal and vocal and remember that 55% of the impact of our communication is based on the visual element and this is lost if you mainly communicate with others by phone! So maximise your positivity through your verbal and vocal communication and the rapport will develop

naturally.

9. Make the other person feel important – it's the greatest desire in human nature. Respect other peoples' position, views, opinions or feelings about things – positively acknowledging someone's point of view doesn't mean you have to agree with them. However, to build rapport effectively, you cannot sit in judgement of others or their opinions.

10. Give thanks! Whether the person has "pulled you up" on something or paid you a compliment, thanking the other person shows humility and gratitude – endearing attributes when building a relationship and developing rapport with others, in both business **and** life!

> *Forgiving someone enables you to stop that person renting valuable space in your head!*

Matching Back – presenting information; a plan of action; the solution

Once you've effectively questioned your customer or caller in a conversational way to establish their needs or wants or requirements, it's important that we **match back** with information or a plan of action or a solution that meets their needs, wants or requirements.

This is where all those little one-percenters that we've looked at so far to ensure a PME are vital to put into use. Remember, words paint pictures, so make sure when you're matching back that you're using positive language to paint positive pictures in the customer or prospect's mind, avoiding those all-powerful RIP phrases that we looked at in an earlier chapter.

Manage customer expectations with the use of the UPOD rule – remember to Under Promise in order to Over Deliver. Give your customer or prospect a sense of choice and control about what's happening by using the Second Option Technique, remembering to give the customer the option **you** would prefer them to take **second** – and change your vocal tone and inflection as you do so. Use all the key elements of your vocal communication to match back positively (and remember that your vocal sound needs to have almost double the impact if you're matching back over the phone and your words need to have over four times more impact.) Ensure your match-back is kept simple and straightforward – remember that KISS Rule, so that when you present information, a plan of action or the solution, you don't use 20 words when 10 will do and you match back in a way that mirrors and matches your customer. Remember too, the power of the WIIFY – tell the customer what's in it for them when matching back with that plan of action that requires them to do something for you, in order to resolve the situation.

If there's a difficult message to convey in the response, then ensure that you apply one of those one-percenters for managing difficult conversation:

- Use the Tape Technique if there's a tad of bad news that you need to give.

- Use the FPQ Technique if there's no good news at all.

- Use the Reframe Technique if you need to disagree with a customer or tell them they're wrong.

- Use the ABC Technique if you need to push back and call the conversation to a close.

These four little one-percenters are all designed to keep the rapport intact, despite the need to communicate a difficult message, either verbally or in writing and this is critical to do when we are matching-back with that information; plan of action or solution.

> *It's true you only have one life, but if you live it right, once will be enough!*

The Corporate Welcome –
a psychological perspective

If you operate within a telephone environment, where creating a great *first impression* is tougher to achieve than when we meet people face-to-face, then you'll be well aware of the need to make the most of those critical first 4 to 14 seconds when a prospect or customer telephones into your company. We are all psychological beings – and there is a fair bit of psychology going on at the other end of the phone at the point of your customer or prospect telephoning you, because they are unconsciously sitting on an emotional matrix, known as the HT-LT Matrix (High-Tension, Low-Trust).

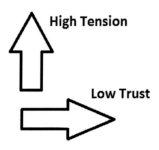

There will be various reasons why your caller is in high tension, none more so than the fact that they can't see you – remember over half their ability to impact you with what they're saying is lost.

Of course, trying to convey your point when you have no visual cues or influences either way is very stressful in itself. Sometimes the person is in high-tension mode because they have a problem they need to solve, or perhaps they've had a problem in the past (God forbid with you!) or maybe they're tele-phobic and they just don't like communicating by telephone.

There will be all sorts of reasons why your customer or caller is in low-trust mode and again, the very fact that they can't see you may cause them not to trust you. Maybe the caller doesn't trust you to do what you say you're going to do, because they speak to many companies just like yours who promise to reply to them and never do – maybe that's been you too! Or maybe they don't trust you because they've had a previous bad experience with a similar situation or (God forbid again) with you!

Whatever the reasons for your customer or caller to be in HT-LT mode and no matter how high or low they are on this emotional matrix, it's important that we recognise, appreciate and respect the fact they're on it.

We only have between 4 and 14 seconds to lower tension, increase trust and create that great first impression, which as you know, we never have a second chance to do. While your customer is waiting to reach you, whether that's via your switch board or your IVR system or simply waiting for you to answer their call directly, they are rehearsing what they want to say to you.

At the point of you answering the phone and accepting their call, they only want to know two things:

1. Am I in the right place?

2. Am I going to be offered some help?

It's critical that you answer these questions at the initial greeting stage of the call so that you can immediately start to turn that emotional matrix on its head, build trust and decrease tension within those critical first few seconds.

How do we do that? We do it by communicating the Voice of our Brand from the outset – a Corporate Welcome that says: "be assured Mr/Mrs Caller, whoever takes your call is a Brand Ambassador for our organisation, where we all sing from the same hymn sheet and do our upmost to create a great first impression from the outset!"

The Corporate Welcome should follow a recipe or structure that ensures you and your colleagues all sing from that same song-sheet, in *one* voice, albeit in your own unique way, because of course, we are all different and the way in which we communicate our corporate sound will be different too.

Your Corporate Welcome is wholly designed to lower tension, increase trust and create a great first impression so it consists of the following steps:

1. **A verbal handshake** – a common courtesy of outstretching the arm to greet your caller with a "good morning," "good afternoon" or a "good evening," (evening begins at 5 o'clock in the winter and at 6 o'clock in the summer) and never a "hello" or a "hi"

2. Your **company** and/or **dept. name** comes next, ensuring that you give your company name a proper introduction because remember, this is one of the questions your customer wants answered in those vital first few seconds, so we need to make sure they hear it. We also need to ensure the company name and/or department name is given in the same way by everyone who answers the phone.

For example: a proper introduction may be "welcome to First Impression Training" or "Thank you for calling First Impression Training" or "You're through to First Impression Training".

3. The **offer of help** is next – and we know from our experience, the best offer of help that you can give is a "How may I help you?" It's far more powerful than a "Can I help?" or "Can I help you? The **how** indicates "in what **way** can I help you?" as opposed to a "Can I help you?" which begs the question "I don't know, can you?" The *you* at the end of the offer of help personalises the question, so that the caller recognises our attention is solely on them at this point.

4. The caller then states the reason they're calling – and we must let them have their say, even if this means we have to wait for the "bubble to deflate". Assuming the call is for us and not one that we need to transfer, we then move to the next stage of our Corporate Welcome, where we use a **certainly** phrase to take control and move into the driving seat, while gently nudging our caller or customer into the passenger seat beside us, using any phrase that instils trust

and confidence, letting them know that **we** are now going to take care of things.

Examples may include:
"Certainly, I can help you with that…"
or
"I can certainly check that for you…"
or
"yes of course, I can deal with that for you…"
or
"sure, I can do that for you…".

5. Then, now we know our customer or caller is paying attention, we can do the **name exchange**, offering our name *first* before asking for theirs or confirming theirs if they've already given it to us.

For example:
"… you're speaking with Marie today, may I take your name?"
or
"… my name is Marie, may I ask your name?"
or
"… you're through to Marie, Mr Brown".

6. If you operate in an environment whereby you need to perform a **security check** (for data protection purposes) then you will need

to ask some security questions at this point in order to access the customer's account, so it's here that you need to make sure you give your WIIFY for doing so.

For example:

"... in order to access your personal records, can you confirm your full name and date of birth, please"

or

"to ensure I'm speaking to the right person, please can you confirm your..."

or

"... to protect your confidential information, can you confirm the first line of your address and post code for me, please?".

7. If necessary, the final step of the Corporate Welcome, before verbally signposting into the call and responding to the customer's enquiry or query, is to **reaffirm the reason** they're calling. It's particularly important to reaffirm at this stage if the caller has "gone off on one" at the start of the call and you've had to make notes on the key points of their enquiry or query because now you can instil even more trust by confirming the information you've heard to prove you've listened and most importantly, understood what they wanted.

This will guarantee to turn that emotional matrix fully on its head by the time your Corporate Welcome is complete, where you would've used those critical first 4 to 14 seconds wisely to create that great first impression.

> *One day… or day one – you choose, you decide!*

The Corporate Goodbye – a psychological perspective

We all know that we don't ever get a second chance to create a great first impression and we also know that any last impression is a lasting one. So our Corporate Goodbye is as important as our Corporate Hello to ensure we communicate the voice of our brand as positively in those final last seconds as we have done in those vital first seconds, *especially* when communicating by phone.

Remember, 84% of your customer's experience is emotional, so we must ensure that we make every customer **feel good** to have spoken with us when they click off the phone or conclude their conversation with us. If they feel good about their experience with us, they're more likely to talk about us in a positive way and refer and recommend us to others and then they're more likely to return to us or stay loyal to us.

Customers will forget what you said, they'll forget what you've done for them, even if you have been a real GEM and Gone the Extra Mile, but they will never forget how you've made them *feel*. Ensure you create a positive and memorable experience for your customer by helping them to feel good about their

116

experience with you, even if it's been a difficult call or a situation that you've had to speak about.

Your Corporate Goodbye should contain three key elements:

1. First, you should **confirm** and **summarise** the discussion and agree any next steps or actions that your customer, or you, need to take.

2. Next (and *only* when it's appropriate to do so) we should ask the "**anything else**?" question, ensuring that it's not being asked in that typical scripted way like those typical call centres ask it! Namely, *"Is there anything else I can help you with?"* which is usually asked in the same bored, monotone way, simply because that's what the script dictates we ask! You need to change the question each time to reflect the conversation that you've had.

   For example:
   "Do you have any other questions regarding…?"
   or,
   "Is there anything else you need to know about e.g. your agreement?"
   or

"Can I do anything else for you while we're on the phone?"
or
"Is there any further information you need?"

3. Finally, we create the **Feel Good Factor** by saying something (anything) that will make the customer feel positive about their experience with you today. You want your caller to sense that you mean everything that you're saying as you say goodbye, so "have a nice day" is **not** a phrase that you'd use to create the feel-good factor!

    You need to sound as though you mean it, so you might say:
    "Thank you for your time today, Mr/Mrs Customer – and feel free to call me if you need anything else. Enjoy your afternoon"
    or
    "Thank you so much for bringing this to our attention, Mr/Mrs Customer; I'll look forward to speaking with you again on Friday with an update. Take care in the meantime"
    or
    "Thank you for taking my call today, Mr/Mrs Customer. Welcome on board and please do contact me if you have any questions or you need any further help with your account"

Win-win communication is all in the hellos and goodbyes, so focus on those first and last impressions that you're creating and I promise you, you'll be remembered for all the **right** reasons. and your customers will remember you to their own customers, colleagues, friends and family too, so it'll be a triple win!

> *Fear is made in the darkroom where negatives are developed.*

The Written Word –
Ten Golden Rules of Netiquette

Everything that we've covered in this book is transferrable to life, as well as to every area and type of business, whether we're communicating face-to-face or over the phone and applies equally to our communication in the **written word** too.

All those little one-percent ideas, tips and techniques that we've applied to our spoken communication can and will make a hundred percent difference to our written communication too – our letter writing or emails that we are creating every working day.

I'm going to share with you our Ten Golden Rules of Netiquette, to ensure that you can create an equally powerful impact with your written word and ensure that you create that PME when customers or prospects read your emails or letters, just as you do through your spoken word.

The Ten Golden Rules of Netiquette

1. Remember, people are glancers not studiers. First and last impressions are vital, so set the scene in the first paragraph and call for action

or a point forward in the last paragraph. As you know, we never have a second chance to create a good first impression and a last impression is a lasting one, so make sure your first and last few words are positive. The subject box should immediately inform the reader exactly what the email is about – a brief summary that attracts their attention, when the reader then skims the email upon receipt.

Follow the KISS principle – Keep It Simple and Straightforward. Don't use 20 words when 10 will do and keep sentence structure and paragraphing easy on the eye and simple for the reader to read.

Apply the dual-readership path principle – bolding to highlight key words or calls for action, underlining specific points of the letter or email or putting certain words in italics. The dual readership principle is also useful for Golden Rule no.1 – making it even easier for the glancer. If your reader is known to you, mirror and match them appropriately, by writing in a style that your reader can relate to and in a language that they can easily make sense of.

2. Remember, words paint pictures. The reader will make sense of the written word through building pictures in their mind from what they see in black and white. Use positive language to create a positive tone and interpretation of the message in writing. Watch out for those RIP phrases like;
"Don't hesitate to contact me",
"Sorry for the delay in replying to you,"
"Unfortunately, I'm unable to confirm,"
or
"I'm afraid that we've had a number of systems problems lately."

Remember to deliver bad news positively, using one of those four little one-percenters, for managing difficult conversation:

a. The Tape Technique: write about what you can do, before you write about what you can't do;

b. FPQ Technique: shoot from the hip, but verbally express how you are feeling about this no-can-do situation first, before rationally explaining the position.

c. The Reframe Technique: you find something to agree on first, then write about what you disagree with, in order to prove your customer wrong, while maintaining rapport.

    d. The ABC Technique: you push back and do nothing more until the customer has committed to doing something themselves.

3. Watch your P's and Q's. Take care with slang and symbols, the e.g. or ampersand sign, clichés and abbreviations. Numbers should always be typed as words if they're used to start a sentence, or they're less than 10. And quotation marks should always be used for directly quoted speech or text. Dashes are good for adding emphasis to the written word and simplifying sentence structure.

4. Use the person's name to focus attention. Precede both good and bad news with the person's name, however be careful with overuse. Remember to spell the name correctly. It's bad enough to say it incorrectly, but it's even worse to spell it wrongly. And of course, it can lead to all sorts of compliance issues if we work within a data-sensitive environment, if we end up sending legally-binding documents that are misspelt with important things, like the person's name, or indeed, sending information to the wrong address.

5. Create those WIIFYs. Remember, if you need the reader to take action of any kind ensure that you communicate what's in it for them in doing so. The power of the WIIFY lies in letting the reader know the benefit of taking action *before* commanding them to do so.

6. Follow that UPOD Rule. If agreeing to any action yourself, in order to manage your customer's expectations and indeed your own stress levels, then learn to Under Promise so that you're always able to Over Deliver. Remember those three little words: **before, by** and **within as** a means of creating flexibility of response times *and* easing the pressure from your busy work schedule.

7. Check it out. Communication through the written word is more concrete than the spoken word, so there is far less margin for error or mistakes. Spell and grammar check everything, every time, but be aware the system is not fool-proof and common-sense checking, using a manual dictionary or thesaurus, may also be required.

8. Beware, once it's written down, it cannot be taken back! If you have a contentious or a difficult message that you need to relay in

writing, then try one of these three routes first.

    a. Pick up the phone instead.

    b. Don't reply immediately. Take time to just gain some control and think things through in a rational way.

    c. Try reading back the email that you've prepared, in a sarcastic tone, out loud. If you can do this, then you need to change your wording before hitting that send button!

9. Perform the daily triage act. When receiving email, remember the golden rule: touch it only once. Do something with it the first time you open it, otherwise you'll waste time skimming repeatedly through the same email, before doing anything with it. Perform the daily triage act and notice how much time is saved: Action It, Delete It or File It. And remember to return emails in a timely manner – it's a simple act of common courtesy and as the saying goes: "What you give determines what you get."

It's worth noting that the tone of an email is misinterpreted 56% of the time, so the best way to ensure 100% understanding is first by face-to-face human interaction, then by phone call or Zoom; Skype; Bomb Bomb or equivalent live link and then by email or other written means. So wherever possible, talk in person, either face-to-face or by phone.

And whatever which way you're communicating, remember… KEEP FIT!

> *When fate hands you a lemon,*
> *make lemonade!*

Conclusion

So there you have it! Showing up and standing out like a PURPLE COW in your particular field is easy peasy lemon squeezy! All the little one-percenters I've shared in this book really can and will make a 100% difference to your customers' experience AND help you to differentiate yourself from others in your marketplace.

It ain't rocket science you know!

We buy into &/or buy from people who we FEEL as though we KNOW, LIKE and TRUST.

Building and maintaining rapport is the golden thread of effective communication to achieve the win-win and when rapport is firmly established, people automatically *feel* as though they know, like and trust you. More importantly, every little tip in this book is designed to achieve exactly that, so give the ideas a go and notice how quickly you're able to communicate as a Brand Ambassador to win the hearts and minds of your prospects and customers.

Remember that 84% of a customer's experience is based on how they **feel** about their interaction with you and your organisation, regardless of the medium of communication. So whether you're providing those Purple Cow WOWS! in a face-to-face setting; over the telephone or through the written word, ensure that you appeal to those emotions – they're processed 24 times faster than logic and rationale after all!

I wish you well in your quest to be the very best.

Remember all you have to do is show up and stand out like that PURPLE COW in **your** field and WOW! *That's* what **your** customers will call SERVICE!

Here's to you - live to delight and be more purple!

Marie X

The UK's Queen of Customer Service
Delivering Purple Cow WOWs! and living with OCD (an Obsession with Customer Delight) day in day out!

As Winnie the Pooh taught us – we can never be more than we believe is possible, so let's start believing in possibilities from this moment on!

Glossary of Terms

FIT
First Impression Training

One-percenter
A simple &straightforward tip or technique that can make a 100% impact

PME
Positive Memorable Experience

UPOD
Under Promise, Over Deliver

WIIFY
What's In It For You?

2nd Option Technique
We give the customer a choice of 2 options, where we make the 2nd option more appealing, to influence the decision WE would prefer the customer to make!

KISS Rule
Keep It Simple & Straightforward

RIP Phrases
Typical business speak or call centre language that we need to 'rest in peace' and find alternatives to

PANEL Method
Developing a Language of Influence to RIP phrasing, by using Positive Alternatives to Neutral/Negative Everyday Language

Golden Thread
This is the skill of Rapport

GEM
Someone who Goes the Extra Mile

Tape Technique
A technique for managing a difficult conversation, where we need to deliver some 'bad news' to a customer – ensure we focus on the good news first!

FPQ Technique
A technique for managing a 'no good news at all' conversation, where we explain how we are Feeling, then explain the Position and then test for commitment or agreement with a Question

Reframe Technique

A technique for telling a customer they are **wrong,**
while maintaining rapport and helping the customer
save face! We find something to **agree** on *first,*
before **disagreeing** with the customer and bringing
on the evidence!

ABC Technique

A technique that allows us to call a round-in-circles
conversation to a close, while maintaining rapport.
The ABC stands for Assertive Boundary Control.

Purple Cow

I love Seth Godin's book, entitled "Purple Cow:
Transform Your Business by Being Remarkable".
and have applied his analogy into those frontline
service conversations we each have every day. In a
field full of black and white cows the purple one is
sure to stand out!

NLP

Neuro Linguistic Programming is the study of
human excellence. It includes communication,
personal development and psychotherapy created by
Richard Bandler and John Grinder in California in
the '70s. Some of the techniques we've shared in
this book have their origins within NLP.

OCD
Most commonly used as a mental health acronym for Obsessive Compulsive Disorder however borrowed throughout these pages to describe my Obsession with Customer Delight.

BUPA
Private medical health insurance provider

FMCG
Fast Moving Consumer Goods or Consumer Packaged Goods are products that are sold quickly and at relatively low cost.

DNA
Short for Deoxyribonucleic Acid – the molecule that contains your genetic code.

MAD
Make A Difference

GAS
When you really Give A Sh*t

PMA
Positive Mental Attitude

BMW
Not the car this time but those people best described as Blamers, Moaners and Whingers.

SAD Syndrome
Seasonal Affective Disorder – type of depression related to changes in the season

Dopamine
Neurotransmitter in the brain – chemical released by neurons to send signals to other nerve cells.

RA-O Factor
Taking Responsibility, Accountability and Ownership as true brand ambassadors.

HT-LT
High Tension, Low Trust Matrix

TED Principle
Tell, Explain, Describe

TRQ
True Response Question

Amygdala
Almond-shaped set of neurons located deep in the brains medial temporal lobe shown to play a key

role in the processing of emotions. Part of the limbic system.

Zoom
Online video conferencing and webinar service

Skype
Free video calling service from Microsoft

BombBomb
Video emailing service provider.

IVR
Interactive Voice Response is a technology allowing computers to interact with humans through the use of voice and tone inputs via keypad.

Netiquette
Combination of the words "network" and "etiquette" and adapted here as a set of best-practice guidelines for written communication.

About Marie Cross

Marie is co-founder of First Impression Training and has over 35 years' experience within the customer-service environment. An award-winning entrepreneur, she has a formidable collection of industry achievements to her name and as a customer-service specialist, Marie has also been called upon to judge a variety of categories at many UK Industry Award programmes over the years. Indeed, she's been proud to "stand on the other side" at the European Contact Centre & Customer Service Awards, when First Impression Training partnered with Legal & General Insurance to claim their finalist accolade for Customer Service Training Programme of the Year and as a finalist at the UK Employee Experience Awards with AXAPPP's SME Broker Sales Team in Leicester.

She began her career with BUPA as a telephone-marketing executive, concluding her time there as a senior training consultant, responsible for the training and development of branch sales and customer-support staff throughout the UK and Scotland. Her wealth of experience across the business spectrum, from financial services to healthcare to FMCG and travel, has enabled her to work in a variety of customer service, sales, sales training, coaching and management roles over the years and her impressive track record has earned her an excellent reputation, both as an outstanding professional and a first class trainer and personal coach within her specialist field.

Marie is passionate about people **and** training – evident in her highly interactive and engaging training and coaching interventions, designed to stimulate and educate everyone she works with. An experienced Life and Business Coach, NLP Master Practitioner and Hypnotherapist, Marie also works in private practice with individuals, helping them to fulfil their goals in order to live their best life. Marie's overall aim is to add real, measurable value to both the individual and the organisation, recognising people as *the* vital ingredient in the recipe for success – she therefore works energetically to bring about the desired changes in behaviour and performance of the people she trains and coaches, wholly committed to developing their potential, regardless of their start point. She firmly believes that we can never be more than we believe is possible, so constantly pushes herself and those she partners to believe in possibilities each and every day!

First
Impression
Training

Web: www.firstimpressiontraining.co.uk

Tel: +44 1622 761321

Email: marie@firstimpressiontraining.co.uk

Facebook: fb.me/firstimpressiontraining.co.uk

LinkedIn: linkedin.com/in/fitmarie

Twitter: @MarieCross_FIT

Marie & the First Impression Training team have been proud to partner many of the giants of British industry since their launch in 2001, including:

FUJIFILM

EQUINITI

Acknowledgements – past & present:

They say that having a bad memory may be hereditary, so if I have forgotten to mention you, please forgive me – and blame my dear old Dad! To everyone who has been involved in this incredible journey of mine, whether you're a customer, colleague, friend or prospect – THANK YOU, from the bottom of my heart:

Andy Gibney & the team at 3P Publishing. My awesome training team – Mags, Dee, Lyn & Mandy. My equally awesome reception team – Jacqui & the Genies. Aarif Merali & his super-creative team at d2rCrossMedia. Nigel Botterill & all the 'family' at the Entrepreneurs Circle. All my EC friends – far too many to mention.

AND MY MUST MENTIONS:

Sue Morris, Jane Kempler, Susie Lotherington, Lindsey Agness, Diana Araujo, Don Hales, Gemma Bailey, Olive Hickmott, Andy Harrington, Gemma Toner, Andy Willcox, Stuart Bevins, Frahana Rashid, Emyr Griffiths, Ian Edwards, Paul McGarrigle, Colin Forster, Clare Harris, Mark Taylor, Wendy Matthews, Linda Wooldridge, Stephen Peattie, Graham Hoskins, Tony Lock,

JoAnne Lancaster, Peter Jolly, Steve Wood, Mike Horton, Claire Jex, John Bishop, David Sheppard, Sara Harris, Nusha Osborne, Gary Dransfield, Arminda O'Reilly, Debbie Clarke, Matthew Rolph, Eddie Ray, Michelle Turnbull, Maria Vidler, Martin Lally, Nicole Wakefield, Jerry Robins, Duncan Simmons, Gary Neilson, Beverly Futtit, Simon Tilling, Vicky Sievewright, Sharon Smith, Lucy Ricketts, Guy Wakeley, Darren Charles, Brian Gilfillan, Gary Robins, Dawn Butcher, Jon Bartlett, Roger Harrop, Julie Griffiths, Jonathan Howarth, Jayne Spencer, Martin Prior, Petie Loyal-Thomas, Mark Stewart, Fiona McLeod, Sarah Sargent, Sharon Wilson, Martin Brealey, Dave Briggs, Chris Rowthorn, Merryn Western, Ramesh Malhan, Mike Fenton, Tracy Riley, Claire Etherington, Matthew Atherton and James Blamey.

AN OFFER FROM MARIE CROSS
For readers *of Make Their Day!*

Dear Reader,

Firstly, thank you so much for reading this book, which I hope has provided you with plenty of insight about the ridiculous ease by which you can make someone's day – in business *and* life.

Now that the reading has ended, the doing should begin, because as we know, ideas don't work -unless YOU do!

So you have two choices now.

You can either place this book on your bookshelf or lend it out or put it in your bottom drawer or somewhere else in the ether – or you can take advantage of the offer I'm about to make to you, which will ensure the 'getting going of the doing' is waaaaay easier for you, so just read on for a moment longer….

In 2017 I began a mission, to somehow lay down and document my life's work, in a practical and useable way, from my days as a telemarketing executive at BUPA, through the terrifying years of nursing a sickly consultancy business back to full health, right

142

up until today - where I feel more fortunate and blessed than ever before to be living & breathing my life's vision, day in and day out.

After many painful weeks and months in the studio and the study, this mission resulted in the creation of our first ever 'product', *FIT Online,* which was launched with our flagship programme: the ***Ultimate Customer Service Training Programme (UCSTP)***

The ***UCSTP*** is an online training programme, which consists of 21 customer service modules, each containing live video training by me and a 62-page practical workbook, where you'll complete a series of activities and exercises with testing at the end of each module, resulting in your very own CPD Accredited Certificate of Achievement.

To find out more AND take advantage of this fantastic offer I'm making to you (as a thank you for reading this book*)* watch the video I've created especially for you at www.maketheirday.today

If you've enjoyed reading ***Make Their Day!*** then I know for sure, you'll enjoy taking part in our flagship programme: the ***Ultimate Customer Service Training Programme*** AND receiving your fully accredited CPD Certificate of Achievement upon completion.

Whatever you decide to do, I wish you everything you wish for yourself – and more!

Here's to your continued success as a Brand Ambassador!

Marie

Offer is subject to change without prior notice.
Small shipping/handling charge may apply.